Cooking Together

Making Memories and Meals

Michelle Day and Eric Bleimeister

iUniverse, Inc.
Bloomington

Cooking Together
Making Memories and Meals

Illustrations by Eric Bleimeister
Cover Photo courtesy Jodi Foley
Eric's Author Photo courtesy Tracey Harrington, TH Photos:
Interior photos by the authors.

iUniverse books may be ordered through booksellers or by contacting:

iUniverse
1663 Liberty Drive
Bloomington, IN 47403
www.iuniverse.com
1-800-Authors (1-800-288-4677)

ISBN: 978-1-4620-1440-8 (sc)
ISBN: 978-1-4620-1442-2 (e)

Library of Congress Control Number: 2011909708

Printed in the United States of America

iUniverse rev. date: 03/02/2012

Many of our friends have helped us along with this project. I would like to dedicate this book first and foremost to my parents, Arthur and Mary Day. Without their love and support this book and my dreams would not be possible.

Please visit us on www.kidsandacook.com

Contents

CHAPTER 9

SALADS

Not just lettuce, but unique salads that any family member can help prepare. Salads are the most expedient way to bring kids into kitchen activities.

CHAPTER 10

SIDE DISHES

A variety of easy, cost effective and nutritious sides that will keep the whole family enticed at meal time.

CHAPTER 11

SOUPS

Nothing is easier to make than soup and the whole family can partake in the activity. Homemade soup is one of the most budget conscientious and healthful meals you can have. Here we show you how to do it.

CHAPTER 12

SNACKS

Your family will never miss those mass produced, processed food snacks when you start making these quick recipes together at home.

CHAPTER 13

SWEET TREATS

Everyone deserves something sweet and these are almost all guilt free.

Author's Note

Cooking with your kids is more than merely making cookies or brownies for some special occasion. Cooking with your children forms a bond that will provide a life time of memories for both you and them. Gathering around the table to eat together has been the cornerstone of humankind since the beginning. Cooking together does not have to happen at every meal or every day. A little help with prep work or input into the selection of food goes a long way. Gently establishing bond over preparing the family meal provides your children with a sense of stability that will carry them over to adulthood and how to raise their own children. Cooking provides useful skills in more ways than just healthful dietary knowledge, as this volume will explain. Cooking together can be established at any age. And since every child is different they will display different preferences and this book provides guidelines for you.

For those of you concerned about diet and what you eat, all our recipes take a health conscious approach to food. You will discover that making things from scratch is no more difficult or expensive than buying pre-packaged goods. Again little changes make a life time of difference.

This new book is packed with useful information, historic tidbits and culinary advice --all of which provide subject matter for you to talk to your kids about. And of course, it shows you how to make delicious and fantastic meals with your children. These are meals that are healthy, easy to prepare and ones the whole family will love.

Preface

Memories are the road map we use to guide ourselves through the seamless roads of our adult lives. For me, my memories were of spending time with my family in the kitchen. We created meals together which have been a guide throughout my life. When I lived on my own for the first time in New York City and I was feeling as if the world was attacking, I retreated to my small galley kitchen and re-created food from home. When I am angry, frustrated, or mad, it's the memories of being in my mom's kitchen with her or my dad, the smells and sounds of laughter that are there to bring me out of my bad day, help to calm my spirit, and make me smile. I think of all the life lessons I learned while with them, the "awkward talks" we had, that never seemed awkward at the time, and still don't today, because I was in a safe, easy, fun environment. The things we would talk about didn't seem so threatening, therefore those lessons stuck with me. Today I find myself calling upon those talks we had while simmering a big pot of stew, or chopping vegetables more and more as I navigate the many twist and turns I go through in my life, I know I am doing something right when my own kitchen smells like my mom's kitchen did.

When it comes to food and children, we either have fond memories of it, funny stories about it, or just plain awful nightmares of it. Any way you look at it they're memories and experiences that have stuck with you. As parents, teachers, guardians, friends, and mentors is it not our job to help build the many memories our children create? Memories that will follow them into their adult lives and give them a safe place to retreat to when they need to. It is up to us as adults to provide them with the foundation that will guide them in to becoming a responsible adult.

This is why I created this book and our website 'Kids and a Cook'. It is why I am passionate about families coming together to make meal time family time once again. If I did not have the memories and solid foundation of family and connection that my parents helped to create for me I know my life would be vastly different, and not in a good way. My words to you the reader are GET IN THE KITCHEN AND COOK WITH YOUR KIDS! They're listening.

—Michelle

Introduction

If the kitchen is the center of the home (which is true otherwise why does everyone congregate there?) Then it should also hold true that cooking is the main essential to family life and the home. **Cooking Together** focuses on being in the kitchen with your children. This book spans kid friendly recipes and more advanced, family oriented and slightly gourmet (yet easy) dishes, which will encourage your kids to try new foods, build excitement when it comes to putting dishes together and learn ways to pair foods with meals. This book will encourage you and your children to learn where food comes from and how it's produced, not only in how you can make a great meal from it.

Kids will be kids. Snacks and sugars in moderation for the average, healthy kid are not necessarily bad. What's important is how you can change their overall diet so that treats will have less an adverse effect (and be more of a treat). After all, treat is not a treat if it's served regularly. It loses its effect as something of importance or a reward.

This Book is More Than Just Recipes! It's about teaching your family healthy eating habits by exploring new foods and augmenting recipes in a manner that will ingratiate children to positive dietary habits. You will find important information about food throughout this book. Cooking with the entire family is fun. In this day and age, when most parents have two jobs, it's the dinner that usually suffers. When children have an interest in making a meal, they are more apt to help either parent. It becomes a terrific way for moms and dads to interact with their kids, build memories, and share the dinner chores and for kids to feel empowered.

Kids need to be active participants and have a say in what they are cooking and eating. It may take longer to prepare meals with their assistance during the beginning stages but that won't last long. Early on they will start out helping and lose interest before the meal is done. That's fine. Keep re-introducing them to meal prep.

When their friends come over on a play date, have those kids assist with making the snacks too (like fruit dipped in either chocolate or Greek yogurt sweetened with honey or agave nectar or smoothies made from fresh and frozen fruits instead of juice boxes). Your children will soon come to think this is the norm because it will become so. The basis is to teach your children that better nutrition is fun and simple to prepare. Kids tend to eat better when they are amongst others. Which is why making healthy play date foods is important. Play dates can play an important role in getting your kids and their friends to eat better snacks. It helps to set up an overall healthy eating program. We've included some recipes in here that kids will love to make and eat with their friends and not even know the nutritional benefits they are ingesting.

—Michelle & Eric

Chapter 1
The Benefits of Cooking With Your Kids

Integrate Healthy and Natural Foods

Real, earth grown, natural foods reduce the amount of additives and chemicals in our diet.

They are not harder to prepare and do not necessarily cost more. Eat what's in season. You'll become less bored with your diet that way too.

Get Your Kids To Eat The Color Wheel!

If you think of the primary colors, or those in a rainbow, you will find that these foods have the most nutrients. Look for food as they appear in nature, not from a processed box. This is a fun exercise and reinforces learning from pre and grade schools. Try getting your kids to pick out fruits and vegetables from the grocery store and make a color wheel.

Try to increase your intake of whole grains. Substitute brown rice, bulgur wheat or quinoa for white rice. With a little seasoning your kids may never know the difference and they won't miss the white rice once they are used to the other stuff. These whole grains are mild and can accompany any main course. They are higher in protein, fiber and nutrients than processed foods and white rice.

Use more beans and lentils too. Legumes are a wonderful source of fiber, vitamins, iron and proteins and can even be added to your favorite pasta and Italian meals. Cannellini beans have a wonderful taste and are great in soups or with sausage. Black beans are bold, spicy and hearty. Red kidney beans (both shades-- dark and light) pair up well with vegetables and meats and in Southwestern, Spanish and Italian inspired foods. They all take to spices and sauces exceptionally well too.

The foods mentioned above require no more effort to make than boiling white rice.

Root vegetables like any of the squash varieties or turnips make a wonderful substitute for potatoes. They have a lower Glycemic index and higher nutrient content. Root vegetables can be less expensive too.

Offer some sort of dark leafy green with meals because foods that can be eaten raw should be included as much as possible. A good rule of thumb is to use food that looks the same when it's grown as it does when you begin to prepare it. That way you minimize over processed or altered foods. For canned or frozen fruits and vegetables the ingredient list should only read what the fruit or vegetable is. And water, maybe.

Pastries and processed baked goods present a difficult challenge to parents. Many of these processed desserts are loaded with too many calories and "engineered" ingredients that just may not be healthful and often are so concentrated that they outweigh the entire daily recommendation allowance. Which is why obesity and other childhood (and adult --for that matter) illnesses have become much too prevalent. With a little knowledge it's easy to make many of your baked goods at home from scratch using better ingredients. And the taste is better, more natural and not hinted with chemicals. Your kids will like them. Our '**Superhero Muffins**' are aptly named for many reasons. I use 100% whole wheat flour whenever I can, not the enriched variety. In the milling process about 60% of the nutrients are stripped from the wheat kernel. Since 1941, the USDA has required wheat flour to be 'enriched' by adding back vitamins such as B1, B2, B3 and Iron. With 100% the bran and germ remain so you get all the natural nutrients inherent in the wheat. Whole Wheat has been shown to help maintain a healthy body weight in women and reduce the risk of Type 2 diabetes and cardiovascular disease, reduce chronic inflammation and even Gallstones. Adding Flax Seed Meal to your flour does little toward the taste but sure does improve the nutritional benefit. Use the Meal, not the seeds since kids might not like the texture of the seeds. (Seeds are very good in salads or added to homemade breads, however). Flax Seed is nature's richest source of Omega-3 Fatty Acid which is vital to the health of all body systems and brain concentration. It' is loaded with B and E Vitamins, high in soluble and insoluble fiber, and Mucilage, which stabilizes blood sugar. Every 100Gms of Flax Seed contains between 25 – 30 Grams of protein. It is a natural laxative, and is excellent to help burn fat and build muscle and reduce water bloating. It's also been suggested that it might help fight acne.

Food Can Bring Families Together

In past generations the entire family was responsible for putting a meal together whether it was an agrarian society or an extended family living in the city or suburb. The work was delegated to the entire clan. As generations progressed we've moved away from this, but many people still have fond memories of 'family meals' or their grandmother's recipes. This heritage you can pass on to your children.

Kids have an inherent love for cooking – why has the 'Easy Bake oven' been popular for so long and why do kids still make mud pies generation after generation?

The Family Meal

Currently, it seems as if the family meal is dying. If this is so, with it an entire way of life will pass. If the family meal is not dying it has definitely hit a crisis point. The family meal is one of the only sources of regular interaction parents have with their kids and kids have with their siblings. It's a way to find out what the other family members did during the day, what is coming up in the near future. The family meal, as we know it, has been the core of society for centuries. It has been so in many cultures and regions since before the written word and probably since man first gathered around a fire in a cave somewhere. It formed the first attempt at community. It is where we share our lives. It is also eroding due to our modern society and its modern pressures.

The family meal comprises the good and bad components of family life, of having to deal with siblings, scheduling, squabbles and ultimately provides that bond that establishes a family. Kids will grouse at being taken away from the TV or video game, but the meal only lasts a short time and it's important. Aside from finding out what is going on, it's a chance to see your children's socialization skills and if they are eating right. There is a reason behind why parents (for generations) sent their kids to bed hungry. It was to teach them discipline and to eat what's on the table. This is easier to do when the entire family (even if it's just you and them) are eating together. More than anything the family meal becomes a mainstay of the daily routine. The structure for the family is based on this routine and offers a sense of order in kid's lives.

Hopefully this book will provide inspiration to stop the erosion of the family meal – at least in your home --and help you make lasting impressions with your kids.

WAYS to Introduce Your Kids to Cooking

You'll need to keep their interest level high by using cooking themes and fun endeavors. Initially kids will want to help, but their interest may wan. (This is OK - just keep including them in some part of the family meal.)

- Get kids interested in what they eat.
- Cooking for kids with allergies and dietary issues- talk to your kids about the children in their class who can't have peanut butter or milk.

- Visit a farmer's market - an inexpensive family trip where kids can pick out foods they find interesting and then prepare it at home.
- Learn where foods come from. Kids love farms, look for places that give tours.
- Teach Safe Cooking techniques and kitchen etiquette.
- Pick one NEW FOOD item with your kids each time you go shopping
- It's 'The Family Kitchen': Clean up can be fun too (and moms will be happy for the help).
- "Make dinner for daddy night."
- "Monday is mom's night off!" Somebody else make dinner!
- Motivate kids with healthy snack food.

WHY Cooking With Your Kids Is Important

- Adults can connect with kids through food.
- Kids discover new foods, facilitating a desire to learn.
- Empower choice.
- Learn to work with people (starting with siblings).
- Strengthen the familial bond.
- Cooking skills improve reading & math comprehension.
- Kids who like to work alongside parents are happier. Children and parents are less stressed.
- Kids like to play with ingredients and make things (why not healthy foods?)
- Preparing dishes at home saves families money!
- Offers structured family time.
- Family recipes are being lost as the generations pass.

Cooking with Your Kids Has Both Short & Long Term Benefits

- Teaches them a lifelong skill
- Teaches age appropriate responsibilities that advance as age does
- Pass along family heritage
- Reduce 'drive-thru' and caloric intake and processed foods in overall diet
- Cooking encourages kids to try healthy foods.
- Kids feel a sense of accomplishment and contributing to the family.
- More likely to eat with family when they helped make dinner.
- Parents get to spend quality time with their kids.
- Kids aren't spending time in front of the TV or computer while they're cooking.

- Kids generally eat less junk food when they're cooking at home.
- Kids who learn to eat well may be more likely to eat well as adults.
- Positive cooking experiences can help build self-confidence.
- Kids who cook with their parents may be less likely to abuse drugs.

Cooking teaches the basics for math. How many kids are sitting in class wondering why they need to learn about fractions? They cannot correlate a reason to learn math. It is boring. And sitting in a sterile classroom listening to a teacher drone on about things does not relate to them (or a lot of them to be fair). However cooking gives parents a chance to surreptitiously teach with visual aids-- not lectures. Kids can interpret this knowledge as being useful for making things. And kids like to be creative. It may improve their math scores because they *understand its daily importance to them*. It becomes more than numbers on a blackboard but relative weights and measures.

Cooking is a great way to introduce children to mathematical concepts *like weight, volume and division. The cost of purchasing ingredients imparts the value of money. As kids get older cooking teaches scientific concepts like what change heat brings to raw ingredients. How different ways of cooking can produce a different end product with the same ingredient; textures, odors, sizes and shapes. The examples go on and on.*

We've only listed some of the most beneficial reasons for introducing home cooking to your kids. The most important reason to cook with your kids is to spend time with them. It doesn't matter if a gourmet meal comes out of it. The interaction is what's most important. And you still get dinner on the table.

How To: The What & When:

Kids need to feel important and have a sense of belonging. Younger kids need to feel like their older siblings are not getting all the glory.

Toddlers: An empty pot or plastic mixing bowl and a silicone spatula will make them feel like they are part of the endeavor. Something as simple as this will start them off in the right direction. To older kids this re-enforces the importance of cooking being family time and the sharing of responsibility.

Preschoolers: Can see how the dishes they eat are put together and get hands-on experience, which is a great way to learn and feel like they are helping out. First let them watch what you're doing and then they can help out with small tasks, like washing fruits and vegetables in a colander, stirring ingredients or setting the table with silverware. As they get older, cracking and separating eggs or measuring ingredients are great tasks.

Tweens / School-age kids: Are at the perfect stage to learn some cooking basics that will help use their math skills. They can combine together ingredients for recipes. This is a good opportunity to talk about what occurred in school that day or talk about nutrition and why you chose the ingredients you're using. Under your supervision they are at the age to learn about basic knife safety and gardening.

Teens: Many teens we see in cooking classes appreciate the chance to improve their cooking skills. They already know the basics of simple meals and hot sandwiches and are looking to expand their talent. For others, this is the age to provide them good preparation for when they'll need to cook for themselves. Whether advanced, intermediate or beginner, teens might be interested in a certain type of cooking or trying different cuisines. Indulge them (and take a class together if they let you) or learn how to make an authentic dish at home. Go on the Internet with them and research the history behind a national cuisine or famous product. It could even turn out be a great social studies homework project too.

It seems obvious, BUT Always choose a time —*when you have time*— for your kids to work with you. If you are feeling rushed, it will not be conducive to a fun event.

The recipes in this book are here to broaden your family's culinary horizons, provide you with ideas, and expand your knowledge about healthy eating. You are the cook. We are not presuming to tell you the 'what' or 'how' and 'which task' for cooking methods and prep work you or your kids should perform. Some recipes are more advanced than others and some lend themselves quite well to children doing most of the work. This is the fun part of cooking with your kids! You and your kids should naturally determine which methods and processes they will be involved with and it will depend on their age, skill level and your comfort zone.

COOKBOOKS ARE NOT SUPPOSED TO BE STATIC VOLUMES ON YOUR SHELF.

THEY NEED TO BE OPENED AND USED.

We've placed a page after each recipe so that you and the kids can write notes and your own memories. Make a variation of the recipe, notate how your kids enjoyed it, what you might want to change or if it was for a special occasion. It's a great page for the little ones to draw on-- thereby creating a memory and for the

older kids to experiment with their culinary craft. So let them go at it. Years from now everyone will be happy you did.

Even starting with making one home-made meal together a week is a great beginning toward reducing your family's overall intake of over processed, high calorie and nutrient deficient food. Making one meal a week together will put your family on the road to better health and develop a better relationship with your children.

HEIRLOOM TOMATOES

Chapter 2
Guide to Cookware

This guide is by no means complete, but we have listed the essentials every kitchen should have to prepare a variety of meals in the most healthful manner possible. Purchasing the best equipment you can afford is important, because quality pieces will last longer and perform better. Performing better means the food will cook evenly, brown quicker, need less oil, clean up better and stay new looking longer.

You don't need every gadget to make healthy meals with your kids. Of course some are fun and by all means if you'll use it or it will help get kids interested, get it. Kids love to play and this element can be introduced in cooking by using useful gadgets. Remember when your toddler only wanted to play with the pots and pans in the cabinets?

Try to avoid 'unnatural' compounds or ones, which the 'safety jury' verdict is still out on like aluminum, plastic, or Teflon. Aluminum on a cooking surface is thought by some to be a carcinogen. Others feel that because aluminum is everywhere, the body will absorb too many toxins over the decades creating a potential health issue. So eliminating aluminum cookware will reduce some of this risk. Plastics and PFC coated containers can leach dioxins and PCBs. Teflon, when overheated, may emit harmful PFOA vapors.

For cookware look for **Stainless Steel** and **Cast Iron**.

Stainless Steel

Is non reactive to food and dishwasher safe. Stainless cookware should be made of a multi-ply, which means the manufacturer sandwiches in layers of aluminum (and sometimes copper) in between the stainless steel cooking and oven surfaces. The layers are what transfers and conducts the heat evenly. Of course the more layers the better (and more expensive).

Cast Iron

Is cast iron. Pots and pans have been made the same way for hundreds of years — by molten iron poured into sand-casted molds. Many of these pots and pans are handed down for generations. You have seen these heavy, ugly black pots and pans in your grandmothers' house. Cast iron is superb and second-to-none at even heating, heat retention and durability. You can still find cast iron that you need to 'treat' or season yourself (Instructions provided), but now most makers sell a 'pre-seasoned' pan, which means that sticking will be much less of a problem. There is also enameled coated cast iron. Those are the ones with the pretty French colors.

Non-Stick

You will need at least one non-stick fry pan or skillet. **When you use it DO NOT use high heat.** The pan may warp and those alleged PFOA toxins could leach into the food or air you're breathing as you stand over the pan. No one is 100% sure if using non-stick is harmful, nevertheless cooking on non-stick does not require —nor can it take— high heat like cast iron or stainless. Non-stick's function is more for cooking eggs and more delicate dishes. There are plenty of alternative non-stick manufacturers that no longer use Teflon. If you have a Teflon coated pan, toss it. It's probably a few years too old by now anyhow.

Essential Pots and Pans.
(In No Particular Order)

Skillet

A skillet is another name for a frying pan. You should get an 8 or 10-inch pan, one being coated with a non-PFOA non-stick coating, for use with eggs, pancakes, crepes, and fish. The other skillet should be stainless.

Cast Iron Fry Pan

I call this 'the cowboy pan' because that's exactly what you see in the old westerns hanging off the chuck wagon. Lodge has been casting these since the 1890s right in Tennessee. If seasoned properly you won't have foods sticking and it can be quite slippery! Why we think you should get one is because they are incredibly inexpensive, they can go on the stovetop, the grill, inside the oven and on a camping trip. They conduct heat superbly well and most likely will never wear out. They get better the more you use it. Tell your boys it's a 'cowboy pan' and they may never want to use anything else. One thing; never use soap to clean it. Use water, paper towels and/or kosher salt to scrub off the crusty bits!

(Tell the boys that's how the cowboys cleaned up and you may get out of doing dishes. Or one dish anyway).

Sauté Pan

One of the kitchen essentials and my *Go-To* pan. A sauté pan has a large cooking area and is like a high-sided fry pan with a lid. The sides are usually 2–3 inches high and straight instead of flared or sloped like a fry pan. It allows you to cook with sauces, fry, braise, and steam and sauté.

Sauté Pan

Is There a Difference Between Sautéing & Pan Frying?

Sauté (the verb) is a variation of frying. It's a method of cooking requiring high heat and some sort of liquid 'fat' to cook with. Both use a dry heat cooking and a 'fat' (usually oil or butter) to transfer the heat of the pan to the food. Sautéing requires little fat and is a quick cooking method. With Pan-frying you use more oil and don't toss or move the food around like you do with sauté. Typically in a pan-fry you use enough oil to reach almost halfway up what you are cooking. Good examples are Eggplant Parmesan or Southern Fried Chicken.

Dutch Oven

A thick walled pot with a tight fitting lid, this cooking vessel has been popular for hundreds of years. The traditional older ones came with a handle to hang over a fire. Dutch ovens have been used all over Europe, brought to the new world during colonial times and went west with the pioneers. Usually made of cast iron, most are now enameled for easier use and beauty. These are extremely versatile and durable. You can roast, boil, stew, bake, braise and fry in them.

Stock Pot

A large, high-sided vessel with a lid basically used for heating water or making soups. The volume is necessary for long cooking without reducing the liquid too much.

Sauce Pan

A vessel with vertical sides about as high as the opening's diameter and with one long handle and a lid. Used for simmering, they do not have the same heat capacity of a Dutch Oven and, ironically enough, are not used for making sauces.

Saucier

This is what you make sauces in. The shape allows you reduce down liquids to concentrate their flavor. The sloping shape also allows you easier stirring to avoid burning.

Roasting Pan

This is one of the few pieces of cookware that is not cylindrical. A roasting pan is oblong; high sided and made of heavy gauge metal. It is normally what you make a turkey, chicken or roast beef in. They can go in the oven or be used to make gravies on the stove top

Utensils

Great tools for kids to use are spatulas, wooden spoons, and whisks, measuring cups, measuring spoons and rolling pins. Vegetable peelers, tongs and basting brushes make excellent secondary tools for kids as they progress. All of these can be used with little supervision and are great training tools to keep kids involved in the process of creating a meal. These are also utensils that kids won't outgrow. As they become more adept, less supervision is required and there are more ways to implement those utensils.

A Note on Materials. Silicone is a superior alternative to Plastic. Silicone has an incredibly higher heat tolerance, is tougher and offers much more versatility. It makes for easy-to-clean spatulas, brushes, mats, cutting boards and other utensils. It won't scratch your cookware either.

Spoons

Wooden spoons are a necessity as well. Purchase hard wood spoons. Soft wood spoons will deteriorate quickly. The best are made of olive wood, which has a beautiful grain and is stain resistant and washes really well. Also good is bamboo or hard maple. You will want to have a few spoons in different sizes and shapes.

SPOONS

Spatula

Silicone spatulas have better feel when scraping a bowl clean and they have a higher resistance to heat. Like spoons it's good to have a few different shapes and sizes on hand.

SPATULAS

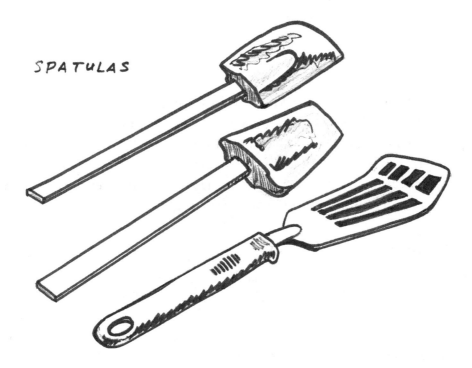

Whisk

You will want to use a whisk for making a sauce, salad dressing or gravy, because an electric mixer is just overkill. Plus, using a whisk is a great way to get your kids to help out, by 'whisking' in the ingredients. This is great learning tool for the young chefs! There are few different types of whisks. The standard whisk is best for eggs, cream and sauces. A balloon whisk (which has a balloon-shaped head) is better for light batters. And a flat whisk gives smoother results.

Tongs

Tongs are essential, since you really do not want to pierce a piece of meat or vegetables. They are incredibly handy to turn food over in a pan turning greens, tossing salads, combining spaghetti noodles with sauce. The list goes on. Try to get one with a spring-loaded mechanism and a lock to hold it closed. Also, silicone tipped tongs tend to allow heavier pieces of meat to slip out, so you want may to consider getting two -- metal and silicone tip. Tongs will end up replacing your cooking forks for almost everything!

Cutting Boards

Purchase high quality, end-grain rock maple cutting board if you can. Treated right, washed gently and periodically wiped with mineral oil it will last you many years.

Your cutting boards need to be non-microbial. You may consider one made from a synthetic or composite compound. They are lighter, easy to clean and can (and should) be put in the dishwasher. When you are preparing chicken, you want to avoid cross contamination with your other foods, so having at least two boards is a real necessity.

Plastic is the least expensive material and readily available. However plastic stains, mars easily and is not as good for your knife as hard wood or a composite. Studies in the mid 1990s lead by Dean Cliver at the University of California's Davis Food Safety Lab show that plastic cutting boards with numerous cut marks actually harbor more bacteria than wooden boards. Plastic allows the bacteria to breed in those knife marks and sometimes-normal hand washing does not kill all the germs, therefore they should be sanitized after every use. The FDA has determined that wooden cutting boards are safe and the wood grain provides a natural defense to bacteria—because it cannot live on the wood and will die off. These findings have been substantiated by recent German and Swiss studies for the European Commission (EC) Hygiene Directive.

The other wood choice is bamboo: a less expensive, environmentally sustainable product which is also naturally bacteria resistant and will not hurt your knives. It provides an attractive and excellent surface for food prep. And don't buy a board that is too small since a larger work surface area is safer.

Never use a glass, marble or Corian-like cutting board-- very bad for your knives and when you are chopping, slicing and cutting these substances can have the same issues as plastic. These materials are for cheese boards.

Vegetable Peelers

There are two basic types, a 'Y" peeler for heaver skinned vegetables and the traditional normal-looking peeler. You can get peelers made with ceramic and with serrated blades both of which work really well. There are many styles of grips. Again, it should comfortable in your hand. Many companies are now making cute peelers for kids.

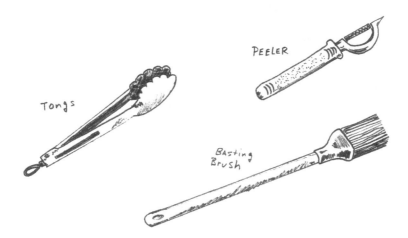

Tongs

PEELER

BAsting Brush

Basting Brushes

I really prefer a silicone headed basting brush and like to have at least two or three sizes. The longer ones are obviously best for grills. Small brushes are very good for kids because they are not so unwieldy and offer more precise control. The silicone rinses off infinitely easier and cleans much better than bristle. Sauces and glazes apply better and silicone does not separate and leave bristles stuck in your food either.

Chapter 3
Guide to Essential Spices and Seasonings

Fresh Herbs

Fresh is best. Fresh herbs, because of their essential oils have a higher concentration of anti-oxidants than fruits and vegetables. A tablespoon of oregano has as much as an apple. Many herbs (like basil, bay leaf, oregano, etc.) have anti-inflammatory, anti bacterial, anti-fungal properties and were used for centuries for both cooking and medicinal purposes. Herbs and spices are a low calorie, no fat, 'real food' and a great way to reduce salt in your diet.

It is the versatility and flavors herbs impart that make them so appealing. You can make nice aromatics if you sauté them a little before adding your main ingredients. You can tie them together to flavor stews or whatever. You can finely chop and use in a dry rub or sprinkle on vegetables for salads and roasts. For sauces, fresh herbs are at their best if added toward the end of the cooking time.

But fresh is not always practical and can be more expensive. Herbs dry wonderfully and store for long periods of time. There is nothing wrong with using dried herbs and for some applications they work better. The flavor in dried herbs is more concentrated and intense than fresh. So you will need to use about 3 times as much of the fresh.

Growing Your Own Fresh Herbs

Your kids will love this. What a great spring and summer project! And it's so very easy. There is little mess and little worry about success. Kids love to choose their own pots and plant herbs in them. Make a day out of it going to the garden center, have them smell the herbs and decide which ones they will tend all summer (or at least plant later in the day). Let them plant their choice in their own clay or plastic pot.

Herbs can be grown in containers, large flowerpots, and of course in garden plots. Herbs do fabulously well in containers because they are hardy and easy to grow requiring little maintenance; just sun, water and average topsoil. A quick haircut to remove the flowers or seedpods in August will keep them bushy and leafy. If you use them frequently pruning might not even be necessary. You will want to plant liked minded herbs together. Which means do not plant rosemary with herbs that like more water.

The herbs I plant in my container garden consist of rosemary, thyme, oregano, chive, parsley, marjoram and basil. I plant a lot of basil and parsley.

I have several large Thermalite (plastic that looks like terracotta) urns that I fill with 1 or 2 of each variety of the herbs I like. I use ordinary topsoil, and fill the pot so that the herbs are planted an inch below the rim. It's OK to put oregano and basil in the same container. Since these containers are on my terrace, I tend to mix for visual interest. I fill the pots with plants, but do not over crowd. They will fill in very quickly. I will plant rosemary in a smaller, separate terracotta pot, which I keep more arid and in full sun.

You can get herbs at nurseries; farm stands and even big box supply houses. The cost usually ranges from $2 to $5 each for plants in 2 or 4-inch pots. These are sufficient in size to start with. When you consider fresh herbs are about $2 a bunch in the market, you can make your money back in weeks by growing your own. And you will have fresh on hand all season -- even into November.

Mint is good in containers too. It is much too invasive in small gardens. You can't get rid of it. Mint is a perennial in the United States meaning that it returns every year and in greater quantity. Mint comes in spearmint, peppermint, chocolate mint, regular mint and many other cultivars. If you have a wild area in your garden, or need it to keep back the edge of woods, plant mint there and leave it alone, except when you want to clip some. Maybe it will keep the poison ivy at bay.

Depending on your zone many of these herbs will 'winter' in the pots.

They say it's best to harvest your herbs in the morning. I don't worry too much about that and cut them when I need them.

Storing Herbs and Spices

There is no need to buy the largest container you can find because the fresher the better, even with dried herbs. They won't last indefinitely. They won't go bad and kill you, but your food won't be as well flavored if you are using 2-year-old dried oregano from the cabinet above the stove. Spices last much longer than herbs.

Store your fresh herbs in a plastic bag in the fridge. Don't tightly wrap them in the bag, let them breathe a little. They should last several days to two weeks. Many fresh herbs freeze well, such as basil.

You can also dry your fresh herbs -- simply by cutting and tying the stems together then hanging upside down somewhere safe and dimly lit. I freeze basil at the end of my growing season (basil will not survive over the winter where I live.) I cut down all the remaining good stalks, and place in my freezer sealed in an airtight freezer bag. When I need a leaf for sauce or pizza I use them whole without defrosting.

Store your dried herbs and spices in a cool, even temperature location. Above the stove is a bad place because of the humidity and heat given off by cooking. Keep out of direct sunlight too. Another reason to buy more often.

Lastly, if you are buying a blended mix, check to see if there is Salt added. I'd avoid purchasing that mix. It becomes too easy to inadvertently get too much salt in your diet. It's good to know ahead of time what ALL the ingredients are. Too much salt (like any single ingredient) will influence the taste. There no need to overdo salt.

Great Garden Herbs Your Family Can Grow

Basil

Extremely high in Vitamin A and a great source of beta-carotene, iron, calcium and vitamin C. Chopping up fresh basil makes a great sprinkle for most anything. You can use the whole leaves too for example --on pizza. Perfect for most dishes, especially anything of with an Italian flare and all meats and chicken. Buy it fresh when you can but keep the dried stuff on hand.

Chervil

A sweet, bi-ennial herb very popular in Europe, particularly France. A great alternative to parsley and dill. It's best used raw.

Chives

Have a sweeter, milder oniony flavor. Great in omelets, salads, baked potatoes, soups. A sense of garden freshness is imparted by using chives. Easy to re-hydrate if bought freeze-dried. (The moisture from salad greens will reconstitute). Excellent to grow in the garden or a container and chives will sprout nice flowers too.

Cilantro

A staple in Mexican cooking it is also heavily used in Asian cooking. It has a unique flavor. It looks a little like Parsley (and often called Chinese parsley) but it is much more pungent. Cilantro is the leaf of the coriander plant. Some people are missing an enzyme in their mouth that makes cilantro taste like soap to them. Try it; you'll know if you are one of them.

Coriander

These seeds have a pungent spicy lemony flavor with sage after tones. It's the seed from the plant that gives us cilantro. But don't confuse the two. They taste different. Coriander is available whole or ground.

Dill Weed

Sweet, bright green fronds usually used in German cooking and in white sauces and potato salads or vegetable dip.

Garlic

Garlic goes in almost everything. You can use fresh garlic, whole, crushed, or minced. Sautéing garlic brings out the aromatics and makes a big difference. I find the minced variety in a jar can be bitter and does not work as well as fresh or powdered.

Marjoram

A sweet, flowery cross between oregano and basil. It offers a delicate woodsy taste and is almost demure compared to oregano. Great in tomato based dishes where you are not looking for a punch of flavor. It is equally as appealing with potatoes and poultry.

Mint

There are numerous varieties of mint cropping up everywhere. Fresh mint is wonderful in drinks, ice teas, as a garnish and in chutneys, salsa and fruit and veggie salads. Great with lamb too. Mint also looks good in tablescapes (the ancient Romans used it for this purpose too) and in flower arrangements. If you plant mint you'll have tons of it -- so use it. Think of all the minty chewing gums when you wonder what mint and its' variations taste like.

Oregano

Sweet, strong pungent and versatile. It is bold, earthy and gusty and not as refined as marjoram. It is high in vitamin K and numerous minerals. A must for Italian-American dishes and meats, fish and chili's and tacos. It's inexpensive and easy to grow and it is one the better dried herbs too.

Parsley

Is more than just a garnish or the green bits your kids complain about floating in your chicken soup. A sprig of parsley is full of flavoniods that contain anti-oxidants. It is richly sweet (not sugary) and actually brings out flavors from the other herbs and spices you used in your meal. You will easily find two of the most common varieties: Curly and Flat Leaf. (The curly is mild, the flat leaf zestier and better in cooking.) Parsley becomes very fresh and beautifully aromatic when chopped.

Use Parsley for cooking in potato or rice dishes, mix with cooked vegetables or salads and of course use it in chicken soup.

Rosemary

A woody, fragrant evergreen perennial herb with needle-like leaves and a pungent pine-like astringent taste. It's a native of the Mediterranean. It cooks exceptionally well with Lamb and Pork and as an addition to Italian dishes. Put the whole stalks on the grill atop a butterflied leg of lamb and watch as the flame flare-ups and propels the fragrance! It's like burning mini-pine trees and the kids will think it's really cool.

Sage

Most stuffing's use sage. That's where you will first remember tasting it. But try this on a baked chicken or turkey -- just lay out the whole leaves on the roast. Sage leaves are grayish and have velvety texture. Its flavor is the perfect enhancement to sausages, cornbreads, muffins, tuna, swordfish, and most roasts meats. With long cooking, sages' assertive flavor mellows nicely.

Shallot

Shallots are likened to a cross between onion and garlic, yet it has a much sweeter, more delicate and complex taste. They're very popular in French cooking and excellent on poultry, veal, and salads. You can buy fresh, they keep as long as onions. A ½ teaspoon of freeze-dried equal one clove of fresh.

Thyme

French Thyme is one of the most fragrant herbs around and another essential. Great for meats, roasts and vegetables. Thyme is excellent because it blends so well with other woody herbs and balances them. Thyme loves to be used in long slowly cooked meals where its essential oils can infuse the dish. So put it in soups, stews, casseroles, and tomato sauce. Its leaves are small so you don't need to chop them and it freezes well. The dried variety is more intense than when fresh.

Tarragon

Tarragon is very floral to the nose and has an assertive licorice taste. Fresh, it is actually more intense than when dried and therefore should be used carefully. It is one of the few herbs you can freeze when fresh and do not need to defrost when you want to use it. Tarragon is most commonly used to flavor pickles, relish and prepared mustards.

Essential Baking Spices

These are the basics you need to bake with. They are essential to create almost every type of baked good imaginable and are wonderful. You will see that many of these spices work well in savory recipes too. I've tried to point out what types of foods works best with each spice.

Allspice

The English, who coined the name Allspice in 1621, thought it tasted like a combination of cinnamon, clove and nutmeg. It is also called Jamaica Pepper, Kurundu and Newspice. A popular baking spice used in pumpkin pie, banana bread and mulled wine in America, it also incredibly important in Island cooking – for jerk seasonings, BBQ sauces and figures prominently in many Middle Eastern recipes. Allspice is a dried fruit, not a blend of spices. The fruit is picked unripe and dried in the sun.

Anise

Anise is Licorice in taste, popular in Mediterranean foods and deserts. You can by Anise ground or in seed form.

Apple Pie Spice

A quick fix for French toast or added to muffins and pancake batter. You can mix up the combination yourself, but on busy morning it is nice to have on hand. Apple pie spice is usually a mix of cinnamons, nutmeg, clove and mace.

Caraway Seed

You see this on Rye bread. It has a very distinct flavor that also enhances cabbage dishes like sauerkraut. It is also very good with fowl.

Cardamom

Originating from India, this spice has become a very popular flavoring in Northern European baking. It is especially prevalent in holiday baking recipes. However in places like India it is a staple in seasoning meats (like pork and lamb) and vegetables. It comes in pods that will keep indefinitely. Ground cardamom is intense and flavorful.

Cinnamon

Everyone knows the taste of cinnamon. However, there are 2 main types of cinnamon and they taste different. The variety from Southeast Asia (Southern China and Vietnam) is spicy-sweet and most familiar to Americans. The strength will depend on the essential oil content and to what grade it has been processed. 'A' being the strongest. 'B' and 'C' are what you will find in Supermarkets. The second variety comes from Ceylon and is less sweet, more complex with citrus overtones and has been popular in British and Mexican desserts.

Cinnamon Sticks

What fun for hot cocoa, coffee and other concoctions. This is perfect for your kids to use to spice up their day. You can also toss a stick into chili, desert sauces and curry dishes too. A couple of scrapes across the stick with a Microplane grater and your kitchen is filled with scent.

Cinnamon Sugar

Is a blend of white sugar, vanilla bean and ground cinnamon. Kids love it on toast, but it is equally as appealing on fresh fruit.

Cocoa Powder

You will find many varieties and qualities of cocoa powder. There are two types of cocoa powder, the first will read "unsweetened Cocoa", generally this is great for all-purpose baking. The second will read "Dutch Processed" these are NOT interchangeable. If a recipe calls for "Dutch Processed" you must use that, not doing so will adversely affect what you're making. "Dutch Processed" is made to temper the acidity of the cocoa bean, and is milder but still smooth and rich with a cocoa taste, and is also where all the beneficial flavonols and anti-oxidants are.

Cocoa powder can easily replace unsweetened baking chocolate; 3 Tablespoons equals a 1-ounce square.

Cloves

Go in everything from a ham to beef to mulled wine and cider and tea. Whole cloves are those tiny blackish balls with sharp edges that people stud citrus fruit and meat with over the holidays. Mainly considered a baking spice it is also widely used in pickling and barbecuing.

Cream of Tartar

Is used to stabilize topping such as meringue and other delicate baked goods.

Ginger

Used in everything from baking (Gingerbread houses, gingersnaps, pumpkin pie) and in Asian and Indian dishes. The root freezes really well and you can shave off what you need when you need it. Powdered form is good for baking. It is also supposed to aid in digestion. The ginger root is available in four different manners, sliced, crystallized, powdered and cracked.

Mace

Is similar to, but much milder than nutmeg. Probably because it comes from the outer layer of the nutmeg fruit. It will impart an orange color to whatever it is used in.

Nutmeg

Nutmeg comes from the West Indies and was once one of the most expensive items on earth. The grated stuff is convenient and easy to use in baking, hot chocolate or coffee. But buy a couple of the whole nutmegs and use a grater. Ten seconds of scraping will give you fresh flavorful nutmeg ready for any recipe that calls for it. And they keep forever --just like a carved wooden knob.

Pumpkin Pie Spice

The name says it all. It's your favorite fall baked goods all in a dried mixture. It's sweet and spicy all at once. This is usually a combination of Cinnamon, allspice, nutmeg, ginger, mace and cloves. Comes in handy if you are limited on space. With a single jar of this on hand you could make killer breakfast muffins at a moment's notice.

Lemon Peel

The zests of lemon are grated or minced and ideal for baking. This is a bright yellow, zesty and springtime fresh flavor. It is available either powdered or minced. The minced version can be rehydrated with a little water. If substituting dried lemon peel for fresh, use about 1/3 of what recipes asks.

Orange Peel

You will find orange peel to be sweeter and less expensive than lemon peel. It's cooking and baking qualities are the same, it just offers the orange taste.

Poppy Seeds

You will find Poppy seeds in a blue or white variety. They have a high, flavorful oil content and go well on rolls, Danish, muffins, fruits and salads. They will become nutty and give off spicy-sweet undertones when heated. They can add a thickness and texture to long cooking sauces. Fried in butter, poppy seed can be added to noodles or pasta and the accompanying sauces for asparagus, potatoes and au gratin dishes. Sprinkled into coleslaw, the seeds give a contrast of both color and texture.

Why You Should Only BUY PURE Extracts

Pure extracts are easy, convenient and actually economical because you need to use so little. Processed without additives, just the citrus, almond or vanilla is extracted into an alcohol base. You get the true flavor, which the less expensive, synthetic extracts cannot imitate.

Almond Extract

Is strong and fragrant and a small amount goes a long way. Usually a 1/2-teaspoon will flavor an entire recipe. It's about 38% alcohol. Fantastic when used for baking cookies, breads, and cakes and in puddings and even some Middle Eastern stews.

Lemon and Orange Extracts

The pure varieties are about 61% pure alcohol and both offer a pure, clean and true fruit flavor. Again you need a little, so use sparingly. Great for baking, candy-making and on glazes or even mixed with sliced fresh fruits.

Vanilla

Vanilla beans come from Madagascar and Mexico. Their flavor is like no other. Madagascar is by far more popular because its flavor is richer and more complex and just better for baked goods. It is considered the standard of vanilla flavor. The Mexican variety is stronger and great in homemade ice cream, hearty sauces or even for homemade vanilla sugar. Whole beans can be expensive so the extract is much more economical. For a whole bean you will want to slice it in half lengthwise and scrape out the seeds. Put the seeds (followed by the bean pod) into whatever liquid (or in a pound of granulated sugar) you are cooking.

Pure Vanilla Extract

Pure Vanilla Extract is rich and complex with a smooth flavor and well worth the investment! There are over 400 flavor components in a good vanilla bean whereas artificial vanilla contains only 1 synthetic vanillin. Vanilla extract is 35% alcohol so it will not spoil. A little goes along way. While it may be exotic vanilla is really easy to use. A tablespoon can really jazz up morning pancake mix and excite your family to get them ready for a busy day.

Essential Cooking Spices

Arrowroot

A clear thickener for sauces and gravies and glazes. Easier to make a slurry from pan juices than Corn Starch because it does not clump as easily.

Bay Leaf

Toss a whole leaf -or two- in a pot of soup or a stew to impart a wonderful flavor. Their antioxidant properties can help in conditions like diabetes, by enabling the body to process insulin efficiently and to treat stomach upsets and reduce the symptoms of digestive disorders because they contain enzymes that help to breakdown proteins and promote digestion of food. Aside from taste this is probably why the bay leaf has become associated with soups, stews and slow cooking meats.

Bouquet Garni

Sprigs of (all or most of) Thyme, Rosemary, Oregano, Marjoram, Basil, Dill, Sage and Tarragon tied to together. This can be dropped into the soup or stew pot or the roasting pan with a bird or joint of beef. Literally that simple, tie them up and toss it in. (Remove before serving).

Celery Seed

An excellent flavor enhancer, it tastes like celery and is a great salt substitute. Generally used in pickling, you can put it in soups, stews and on large cuts of meat or in a Bloody Mary.

Cumin

Worldwide, cumin is the second most popular spice next to black pepper. Use it in everything where you want a nuanced, well-balanced heat and depth of flavor without a burning bite. Known in America for Tex-Mex food, use it in Indian, Asian or on a big piece of meat. You can get it in seed or ground.

Curry

Not all curry is hot. Curry powder is a blend of upwards to 20 or more spices. Indian regional preference determines the flavor and heat index. Curry can be anywhere from sweet, with a rich flavorful bouquet, to fiery hot or somewhere in between. Like chili peppers, curry powders run the entire range of heat and spice and bears culinary investigation. Try them as a seasoning on foods you already like for a great change of pace.

Dill Seed

Use it for pickling. Otherwise you probably don't need it.

Fennel

Fennel is a vegetable often eaten raw (especially by Italians) to cleanse the palate between courses. Fennel contains potassium, vitamin C, fiber, folic acid, phosphorous, iron, calcium and other vitamins. You can use fennel's anise flavor to boost fish dishes, season pork, or add it raw to salads. Fennell tastes like mild licorice and acts as a digestive aid to settle your stomach. The seeds are used in sausage and to season tomato sauce and in baked goods. It is popular throughout the world showing up in European, Chinese and Indian recipes and has been in regular use since before the Romans.

Herbs de Provence

A combination of the sweet French herbs, the floweriness of lavender, the cleanness of fennel and savory Italian herbs. *Herbes de Provence* contains a mix of basil, rosemary, cracked fennel, thyme, savory, tarragon, dill weed, oregano, lavender, chervil and marjoram.

Italian Herb Mix

A blend of oregano, basil, marjoram, thyme and rosemary. Get good quality stuff otherwise it can be bitter. Because it's a blend of herbs not all brands will taste the same. If you find a brand you like, it's great sprinkled on meats, roasted potatoes or pizza, for example.

Peppercorns

Pepper is the number one spice in the world offering the greatest amount of flavor to the widest variety of dishes. Even the finest is affordable.

Depending on how it is harvested and dried, peppercorns can vary in flavor and richness. Most peppercorns you will see are black. You can also find green and pink and white. All of these have a slightly different peppery taste. Green is harvested while the fruit is immature. It will taste peppery with a fresh clean overtone. Peppercorns ripen at different intervals and therefore are still harvested by hand in a centuries old tradition through India and Borneo.

Fresh cracked pepper is wonderful. Add it to your meals at the table and when you are seasoning them on the stove.

White Peppercorns

Are allowed to ripen more than the black and then the dark outer shells are removed. Its taste is a little more subtle, yet still has a rich and winey, slightly hot flavor. White is a nice touch if you need a peppery taste and do not want black sprinkles all over something, i.e. creamy soups and dips.

Paprika

Comes from the capsicum annum pepper. The bright red version is sweet and the darker it gets the more pungent and hotter it becomes. Paprika imparts a bright color and a unique flavor. It's not like a chili pepper in taste. It is almost a signature ingredient in Slavic dishes. Look for sweet and hot varieties- some of which can be very fiery. You will also see it as Hungarian Paprika.

Smoked Spanish Paprika

Pimiento peppers are slowly dried and smoked over oak fires giving this an entirely different flavor than Hungarian paprika. It has a luscious red color and a sweet, cool, smoky taste. Essential in authentic Spanish cooking, you will find it in chorizo sausage, for instance. There are mild, bittersweet and hot varieties. Most smoked paprika will not assault your taste buds but offer a mild bite perfect for shrimp, fish, pork, potatoes and soups and stews.

Tumeric

Tumeric is an orange-yellow spice with a tangy peppery mustard- like flavor which is popular for thousands of years and is used in many curry dishes. Tumeric is also good with eggs, lamb, chicken, sauces and many vegetables. It lends a beautiful color to whatever it is used in.

Wasabi

The bright Day-Glo green mustard from Japan. It's Hot and has a nasal clearing intensity that is unique in that it dissipates quickly without a burning aftertaste. Wasabi is the root of Japanese horseradish, which has been finely grated and formed into a paste. Wasabi is most commonly served alongside sushi or sashimi, but you can use it to flavor beef.

Salt

Salt is Salt is Salt.

Some is just better to cook with. Salt has been glamorized lately, and there has been misinformation about its health benefits. While salt is essential in cooking, **as a flavor enhancer**, it is also pertinent to realize adverse dietary effects of overusing it, especially over a lifetime.

Kosher Salt

There is no Nutritional or chemical compound difference between kosher salt and table salt. It is mined from the same inland deposits as table salt. Because it is coarse, not finely ground like table salt, it is easier to regulate how much you are using and works better in cooking. The size and shape allows it absorb more moisture than other forms of salt which makes it better to cure meats. Hence the 'kosher' terminology; this is the type of salt used to make meat kosher.

Sea Salt

Is harvested from seawater through evaporation. It is about 98% pure salt. The other 2% contains trace minerals that people believe enhance and affect the flavor. This is why you find Sea Salt from all over the world proclaiming its unique flavors. I do find it more flavorful and better to cook with than table salt and it allows me to use less. There are generally no additives --which you may find in table salts.

Sea Salt is primarily a finishing salt, whereas Kosher Salt is a cooking salt.

I use table salt for boiling pasta (since it is inexpensive and most of the water goes down the drain) and in a shaker on the dining room table.

*

Citrus Juice and Zesting

The zest is the outer most part of the rind on any citrus fruit. It is intensely yellow, green or orange. The white part is the pith and that is usually very bitter and should not be used when cooking. Both these parts form the skin or peel and protect the fruit. The zest contains essential oils that has a strong citrus flavor yet does not change the chemical makeup of a recipe by increasing liquidity or acidity. Lemon goes extremely well with either sweet or savory foods.

You should always wash and dry citrus fruit prior to Zesting to make sure any chemicals or waxes are removed. Purchase a Microplane for easy Zesting and Grating your citrus fruits. If you need a peel, a paring knife will do the trick.

We all know citrus fruit is loaded with Vitamin C, but there are many other benefits. Here's why you shouldn't throw your peels away!

Lemon Zest

High in Vitamin C and antioxidants. Lemon zest is an extremely useful seasoning. You bought the fruit already, why not use the outer layer of the peel?

Orange Zest

Is a good source of pectin and contains a unique flavonoid called hesperidin which helps lower cholesterol, acts as an anti-inflammatory and beneficial in the fight against cancer and bone loss. Interestingly, hesperidin is found abundantly in the peel, much less so in the fruit.

You can add lemon or orange zest to many dishes, like rice, couscous, oatmeal, grains, Marinade, salads and salad dressings as well as breakfast cereals or smoothies to help boost the nutrient intake. It's a very good way to make sure your family gets the 5 servings of fruits and vegetables each day.

Limes

Those little green limes have that zingy sweet, tart taste can be interchangeable with lemons in many dishes. Limes are high in vitamin C and ascorbic acid that helps fruits and vegetables from discoloring when exposed to oxygen.

Pure, fresh squeezed juice does not have the bitter flavor you will find with concentrated juices, plus it has all the nutrients of fresh citrus fruit.

It actually does make a difference in what you're cooking.

How To "Supreme" Citrus Fruit:

- Slice of the top of the fruit.
- With a sharp Chef's knife, begin at the top of the fruit and slice downward, following the natural curve of the fruit, cutting away the skin and white pith. You will need to make numerous passes to get around the entire fruit. What you will have left is the beautiful flesh of the fruit.
- Over a bowl, use a small paring knife, section out each segment of fruit, cutting away the internal pith. You will see the natural segmentation to give you a guide where to cut. When done only the clean piece of fruit is left. Squeeze into the bowl whatever juice is left in the pith and discard. (You can save the skins for zesting.)
- This step is necessary for two reasons. 1) Presentation; the pithy membrane is not appealing. 2) The pith is bitter and no one (especially kids) likes eating it.

Chapter 4
Healthy Homemade Salad Dressings

It is incredibly simple to make homemade dressings. As you read this cookbook you will see that most of our recipes call for the same essential ingredients you need to make your own homemade dressings.

Good dressings are versatile and can be great for dips and on potatoes and pasta salads. There are so many things you can do when you make your own dip. Obviously homemade dressings are fresher and they allow your family a chance to experiment.

You regulate the contents too. It's a way to make a much healthier dressing and use a lot less pre-processed foods and ingredients. When you think about the amount of calories, salt and fat in mass marketed creamy dressings, they can actually make vegetables unhealthy!

Here are some average calories in store bought salad dressings:

Caesar Salad Dressing (1 tbsp) contains 70 calories
Ranch Salad Dressing (1 tbsp) contains 85 calories
French Salad Dressing (1 tbsp) contains 60 calories

You can get light varieties with fewer calories, but have you tried reading the ingredient lists? I'm not saying to never buy prepackage dressings. Just be cognizant of how much you use and what's in it. Even if homemade is better, sometimes you just want something different – or quick. Hopefully this book and our website *Kids and a Cook* can help expand your family's culinary horizons and improve your overall dietary choices. Food is supposed to be fun and enjoyable as well as nutritious.

To make our own dressings you really only need the following: **High quality Olive Oil,**

Vinegar, (you can also experiment and pick up **White Wine Vinegar, Apple Cider vinegar,** and **a Balsamic or Sherry Vinegar** too), **salt, dried herbs, garlic, dairy products** (you'll never have to wonder what to do with left over Buttermilk again), **fresh lemons** and **fresh herbs**. Again these are really basic ingredients for most recipes. Buy a couple glass bottles to keep the unused dressing in.

Which means your salad dressings could cost you relatively nothing!

A Note About Dressing Salads

The dressing isn't the only flavor you should taste. Dressing should lightly coat the salad leaves, not drench them. It should bring out the flavor of the greens and other ingredients. You don't want to wilt the greens or make everything soggy. There shouldn't be a pool of it on the bottom of the salad bowl. That's wasting dressing anyway and you don't need the extra calories, fat and salt. I have been guilty of overdoing dressing too. It's an easy slip of the hand. It seems even most restaurants will over use the amount of dressing and subsequently kill a decent salad. Maybe that perpetuates the heavy-handed use of dressing at home. If your favorite restaurant liberally pours it on, it must be proper. In fine restaurants, with a talented Sous chef, you will see a very light touch of dressing upon the greens. It is just enough, more than a hint, never overpowering, to bring out the nuance of the dressing's characteristic to enhance the type of greens used.

You can do this at home easily. One, make sure you have a shaker top or spout if you are using bottled, or bottling our own. Two: mix the dressing in a separate small bowl and spoon it on top of the salad, tossing as you go. I like to use the baker's "folding" method where you literally grab the greens and fold them over each other, turning the bowl as you go, instead of flipping everything around. This thoroughly mixes my greens and dressing without bruising. Leave the balance in the small bowl and set on the table. (In case you were too stingy).

Here are a few, very simple, classic family dressings.

Buttermilk Ranch

Buttermilk gives this dressing the body and flavor it needs and keeps the fat content lower than in most dressing. And its great way to use up that quart of buttermilk you bought for 1 recipe. You can use this dressing as a marinade for chicken or fish too. This dressing is little more than buttermilk and mayonnaise with herbs. It's become the number one dressing in the United States. (So they say. Who's to really know?) Nevertheless it easy to make and tastes good.

Ingredients:
- 1 Cup Buttermilk
- 1/2 Cup Mayonnaise (or plain Greek Yogurt)
- 1 tsp Lemon Juice
- 1/8 tsp Paprika
- 1/4 tsp mustard powder
- 1/2 tsp Celery Seed
- Black Pepper (to taste)
- 1 Tbsp Fresh Parsley, chopped
- 1 tsp Fresh Chives, chopped
- 1/4 teaspoon of dry dill (or a teaspoon chopped fresh)

Whisk or blend all ingredients together in a bowl. Transfer to a bottle and write the expiration date of the buttermilk on the bottle. Depending on desired thickness and what you want to use it for; you can play with the ratio of buttermilk to mayo or yogurt.

Green Goddess

A venerable classic creamy dressing with overtones of basil and dill is great in dips, with fish sticks and of course salads. There are frighteningly many version of this recipe, which just proves its versatility and popularity. I like to use a mashed avocado to improve the nutrient quota and change things up a little.

Ingredients:
- ¼ Cup Real Mayonnaise
- 1/2-Cup Plain Greek Yogurt
- 1/8 cup Scallions, finely chopped
- 2 Tbsp. Dill
- 2 tbsp. Basil
- Pinch of Celery Seed, Sugar, and Garlic Powder (or 1 clove, minced)
- 1 Tbsp. White Vinegar
- 1 Avocado (optional)

If the herbs are fresh chop them really well, but avoid bruising. Whisk all of the above together, or put in the blender or food processor—more of a necessity if you are adding the avocado. Add a little water if it seems too thick for salad dressing. Taste and determine if you feel you need extra seasoning. If it seems bland to you, add a pinch of salt or lemon juice or extra celery seed. Refrigerate till ready to use.

Italian Vinegar and Oil

It's so simple. The difference between regular Vinegar and Oil and Italian Vinegar and Oil are the spices. And those are spices that you have on hand because you use them for so many recipes. Simply blend in olive oil and white vinegar about 2/3 oil to 1/3 vinegar. Sprinkle in your herbs of garlic, oregano, basil, dried pepper, rosemary, marjoram and thyme (dried works well for this application). Red pepper flakes make a good addition if your family likes spicy! You will have to go by taste, and keep adding until you to get it to where you like it.

Ingredients
- 2/3 Cup Olive Oil
- 1/3 Vinegar (your preferred choice)
- 1 tsp. Garlic powder
- 1 tsp. each: Oregano, basil, black pepper, rosemary, marjoram, thyme
- 1 tsp. Honey or sugar (optional)

To make a creamy Italian version add a ½ cup yogurt or sour cream.

Michelle's House Dressing:

Ingredients
- 2 parts Extra Virgin Olive Oil
- 1 Part Champagne Vinegar
- Salt and Pepper to taste
- 2 Tbsp Dijon Mustard
- 1 Tbsp Sugar

Shake all ingredients vigorously in a sealed container; lightly dress your salad just before serving.

Note: 2 parts to 1 part means if you put in 1 cup Olive Oil you would use ½ cup Vinegar whatever the amount of oil you use put in half that for the vinegar, of course this is subject to taste, if you like more vinegar, use more vinegar. This recipe is quick, easy and can be made in any amount you need.

Cool Blue Cheese Dressing

You need something to dip those spicy hot wings in (see our recipe under snacks). You can serve it up alongside tacos and burritos and as a topping for vegetables or with a spinach salad (add some bacon and a couple hard boiled eggs to the greens). Why not make a healthier version of the tired old stand-by ranch or blue cheese dressing? The dressing is best made up well ahead of time. It should sit for a minimum of an hour before serving. Overnight is even better. The good news is the left over dressing can be put to a lot of uses over the next few days, so it's very economical. I'm recommending Greek Yogurt (instead of sour cream) to add protein rather than fat into this dip. Since you are not cooking this, you will keep the active cultures alive, which can aid digestion and provide immune system support along with the extra calcium.

Ingredients
- 1 Container Greek Yogurt (8 oz.)
- 8oz. Blue Cheese, crumbled
- ¼ Cup Buttermilk
- ¼ Cup Fresh Parsley, minced
- Worcestershire Sauce, to taste
- Kosher Salt & Fresh Ground Pepper, to taste

Simply stir the yogurt up. Then add the Blue Cheese (crumble it into small pieces), Parsley, Worcestershire Sauce, Salt and Pepper and mix. Slowly add the buttermilk, stirring as you go. You do not want to loosen the mixture too much, -- so you may not need the entire amount. Cover and refrigerate until ready to eat.

Chapter 5
Some Very Special Foods
(Kids Don't Eat Enough Of)

AGAVE NECTAR

Agave Nectar has become very popular in recent years. It's been touted as a health food and a great alternative to sugar. It sounds kind of Exotic and mysterious and since it comes from an exotic location it should have some fantastic health secret. Many food manufacturers go to great lengths to get consumers to believe that they went far and wide to finally discover some rainforest plant that has exceptional nutritional value. I'm not saying it's not true; just do your own research.

Well, Agave Nectar is not bad for you. It is syrup made from the Agave plant grown in Mexico. It is the same plant that gives us Tequila.

Agave Nectar is 90% Fructose and does have a relatively low Glycemic index. It is much sweeter than sugar. It is higher in calories than sugar and more expensive. However, you need to use much less. Agave Nectar is processed so it is not a raw food like honey. The processing refers to the nectar's extraction method. Without going into extreme detail, the Juice is extracted from the core of the Agave plant (*the pina*), filtered and heated into simple sugars. The hydrolyzed juice is then concentrated into syrup.

Most Agave Nectar I've found is labeled "organic" and it's only ingredient is agave nectar. At least its' one way to avoid High Fructose Corn Syrup or man-made additives. Agave Nectar in its natural form is lighter and sweeter than honey. There is a light variety which does not alter the taste of food (only sweetens) and the amber imparts a more distinct taste. It has fewer calories than corn syrup products. Many companies are now adding flavors to the nectar. I think this is just a marketing trick. Why not just use real maple syrup if you want maple flavor or blueberry syrup for blueberry flavor? If you are buying flavored Nectar, I would strongly recommend reading the label. You might want to know if the flavors are chemical or natural.

There is nothing wrong with Agave Nectar; it's about as 'bad for you' as sugar is. Which means it's fine used in moderation, and by people without major health conditions or dietary issues. It is a good alternative for people with concerns about glucose intake. It works great on --or in-- anything you would add processed sugar or honey too.

HEIRLOOM TOMATOES AND HERBS

Get them while you can! The homegrown /farm stand tomato season is a really short one. These should not be missed. Whenever you can, buy Heirloom Tomatoes instead of the standardized mega market variety-- if only for the taste (which is reason enough, no need to mention supporting local farms and eating fresher foods).

Heirlooms are hard to get in mega markets because they are thin skinned and hard to commercially stock, the variance in their size, sprawling growing habits (don't do well in cages) make them difficult to efficiently package and price. Additionally Heirlooms must be open-pollinated by natural methods (again effecting commercial efficiency, cost and productivity).

Heirloom Tomatoes are colorful, ranging everywhere from green to purple and black to red. They are dented, ugly, striped, misshapen and not uniform in size or variety. There are too many varieties to name. It is best to buy an assortment and slicing up a variety provides a wonderful nuance and extremely flavorful salad.

But what is an Heirloom Tomato? Truth is, there is no solid definition. They could be from seeds that are 100 years old or from the World War II era, or simply seeds handed down a couple of generations. Besides being open pollinated-- one thing is sure in an Heirloom Tomato; there is no GMO (Genetically Modified Organisms).

All Tomatoes are rich in Lycopene. You may find it interesting that some studies show that when cooked they contain higher concentrations than when raw. They are also rich in vitamins B and C and iron and potassium.

So – Get your kids and visit a Farmer's Market when the summer season starts and get there often! Bring some friends too because running around a farm stand or a multi-venue market is cool. Bringing kids to a local farm, especially where there are animals and pastures is an important experience in a young person's life and you will have a good time too. Have the kids pick the coolest tomatoes they can find. It will be fun when you serve them up with dinner.

WINTER SQUASH AND PUMPKINS

Just what is the difference between winter squash and Halloween pumpkins?

We get this question all the time. There is no botanical distinction. They've been around and cultivated for so long nobody knows from where they originated. Your typical Jack O' Lantern is a variety of squash. Albeit a less tasty one. (The seeds are excellent roasted, but most people know that.) The ubiquitous orange pumpkin is primarily grown for decoration. The larger the orange gourd the more mealy and tough it will be. Use smaller 'sugar' or 'pie' pumpkins for cooking. Substitute acorn or butternut squash and any recipe calling for 'pumpkin' will taste better. Winter squash is versatile. You can bake them, roast them, fry them, boil them and puree them. They are spice friendly and can be prepared sweet or savory.

Winter squash are categorized as the heavy and dense squashes harvested in late fall. They keep for months properly stored. They come in many shapes; sizes and some are downright scary-looking without having to carve ghoulish faces into them.

Winter squash are very rich in B1, B6, folic acid, pantothenic acid, fiber and niacin. They are an excellent source of carotenes which have been shown to reduce the risk of lung cancer, heart disease and Type 2 diabetes. Since Winter squash are heavier than summer squash (because of summer squash's higher water content) they are also more nutrient dense.

Delicata

A great grower for the home garden, these yellow squash have broken green stripes running across their oblong body. It has a sweet and delicate flesh sort of like corn and sweet potatoes.

Hubbard

This one looks all gray-green and gnarly with a ghostly pallor. These are large squash and make excellent autumn and Halloween decorations because of this look. The flesh is bright orange and has a fine texture that is excellent for baking. However these are usually so large and keep so long (because of the thick skin) that they are regulated to decorating. Varieties of Hubbard also come in dark green and orange. You will recognize a Hubbard because of its size, warty skin and oblong shape with a bulbous middle.

Spaghetti

A pale yellow squash whose sweet flesh is the same color as it's' skin. If not over cooked it will have a texture similar to cucumber. This is a great vegetable alternative to pasta (hence the name). Its rich in vitamins and tastes excellent mixed with garlic and a little salt and butter. You can even cook it in the microwave. When cooked, scrape out the flesh with a fork to form the spaghetti-like strands.

Sweet Dumpling

These are shaped like small pumpkins, but they are white with green stripes. It's another great fall gourd decoration, but it is probably one of the best tasting, sweetest winter squashes around. They store for months and make an excellent self-contained container, which can be stuffed and baked. Preparing sweet dumplings this way is a fun project for kids- (even if they won't eat it). Each sweet dumpling is perfect size for a single serving.

Sweet Dumpling

Turban

Turban Squash originated from North America and the Algonquin Indians named them *'Askoot Asquash'* which means 'to eat green'. So I guess the 'eat green' movement has been around for a while.

Their resemblance makes it obvious why we call them 'turbans'. They are also nicknamed a 'Mexican Hat' because of their shape. It has a brim-like bulge under a round top. It is very colorful too, having deep greens with fiery orange and red scattered through the upper portion of the squash. Although considered a winter squash because of its thick skin and storable longevity, it is available all year. Most people consider this a gourd and just use it for decoration! It tastes fine however, some say slightly reminiscent of hazelnut, and can be used in recipes that call for a sugar pumpkin or buttercup squash. Turbans are quite good baked in pies, cakes or muffins (to boost nutrition) or pureed for soups because their flesh becomes velvety. If you are using them for cooking get the smaller ones because they are sweeter and less stringy. The big ones look great in an autumn table scape or on the porch with pumpkins.

Turbans are high in protein and low in carbs and calories (100g has about 37 calories, 8 g. of carbs and 8.8 g. of protein) plus they're loaded with calcium, magnesium, phosphorus, potassium, and vitamins A, B and C.

They are simple to prepare. Simply cut in half or in wedges and remove the seeds and filaments. Drizzle with oil or butter and a little salt then bake at 450 F for about 35 -45 minutes or until the flesh becomes soft and begins to caramelize. You can cook them in a microwave too. Clean and pierce holes in the skin and place in a microwave safe container — skin side up. Cover the prepared pieces with plastic wrap and cook for 10 – 20 minutes (every microwave is different).

Varieties of Winter Squash

Acorn, Banana, Butternut, Buttercup, Carnival, Delicata, Gold Nugget, Hubbard, Kobocha, Spaghetti, Pumpkin, and Turban. The list can go on forever it seems. These are in most markets and many are available all year, although fall and winter will offer the most abundance.

ACORN Sqaush

Quinoa

This wonderful food deserves a special note of explanation.

But what is quinoa? (Keen-wah) Many people still are unaware of the super-powered food originating from Peru. It is a better alternative to rice and potatoes. Quinoa is actually a seed. It's considered grain-like because of its cooking properties. It was staple food for pre-Columbian Andean civilizations, along with maize, for the last 6000 years.

Its protein content is very high (12%–18%), making it a great choice for vegetarians. Quinoa is gluten-free, easy to digest and in high lysine (which is a benefit over wheat or rice.) Barley, corn and rice have less than half the protein content of quinoa. Some wheat comes close, but since quinoa is gluten free it offers an edge if wheat tolerance is an issue. Quinoa contains a balanced set of all 8 essential amino acids, which makes it a complete protein source. It is loaded with dietary fiber, phosphorus, calcium, iron, vitamin E, some B vitamins and magnesium. With this nutrient make-up, it is very important to adults and especially growing children. For instance, about a ½ cup provides a child's daily protein intake.

Quinoa comes in variety of colors but you will mostly find either white or red quinoa. Both have a mild, slightly nutty flavor. Quinoa is wonderfully versatile and can be mixed in casseroles, pilafs, and soups or with a breakfast cereals like oats, or flakes and fruits. Store your quinoa in the refrigerator.

Recipe Tip:
Quinoa is prepared almost identically to white rice. Bring 2 cups of water to a boil with 1 cup of quinoa (and maybe a pat of butter). Stir and reduce heat to a simmer for 15- 18 minutes until the germ has separated. Let stand another 10 – 15 minutes and fluff with a fork. When cooked, quinoa looks like a little curlicue and should offer an *al dente* pasta feel in the mouth.

Cauliflower. And Other Great White Foods

We've all heard that you should buy food that is bright in color and that darker is better (because of a higher nutrient content). At *Kids and a Cook* we've said this ourselves because it is true. However there are some foods that break this rule.

Cauliflower, like other white vegetables, onions and garlic, is **a good source of allicin. (Allicin has been touted as garlic's cure-all). Cauliflower is also a good source of potassium**, selenium, Vitamin C, Folate (a B vitamin) and indole-3-carbinol. These elements and vitamins have been shown to help fight cancer, inhibit tumor growth, free radicals, reduce stroke risk, promote healthy skin and reduce the effects of toxins that the body absorbs on a daily basis by just living our lives. Plus it is a hearty cruciferous vegetable and does more than help detoxify your body --it acts as a tummy filler.

* Cauliflower blends easily into soups, especially puréed soups, mashed vegetable dishes, and casseroles.

Cauliflower with Tumeric

An important step in cooking cauliflower (and broccoli) is too cut the florets off the stems and let them sit for 5-10 minutes. When cruciferous vegetables are cut phenethyl isothiocyanates occurs (this is what allegedly suppresses cancer growth). It stops when they are heated.

Tumeric, an orange-yellow spice with a tangy and peppery mustard-like flavor (used a lot in curry dishes), has also been shown to fight cancer and reduce stomach ailments. It has been used for such things in the Far East for thousands of years. Tumeric is also good with eggs, lamb, chicken, sauces and many vegetables.

Here's the interesting part --there have been studies showing that the pairing of cauliflower with Tumeric increases both substances' health benefits exponentially. Even if that isn't true, the two make a wonderful combination.

Of course when you add Tumeric to cauliflower, they change color and begin to look like some Midwestern popcorn or cheese puff! That might just be enough to fake out the kids to try it.

Recipe Tip:
I like to blanch a head of cauliflower for 5 to 10 minutes then drain and transfer to a roasting pan. Drizzle with olive oil and sprinkle with kosher salt and a healthy dose of Tumeric. Roast for 15 minutes at about 450 degrees, until the edges of the florets are starting to turn brown. Blanching isn't necessary if you have 40 – 45 minutes to cook. Then just roast the prepared florets.

Fennel

Fennel is a bulbous vegetable whose stems and leaves can be eaten raw --to cleanse the plate-- or cooked singularly (sauté them with onions for a healthy side dish) or mixed with other ingredients. Its great added to salads, casseroles, soups or fish dishes. From one vegetable we get two distinct and incredibly versatile culinary products. The stalks and leaves are a vegetable and the seeds are a long-lasting spice. And what a curious little seed it is. These seeds have a mild anise flavor. Yet when they are lightly toasted they become downright spicy. Fennel seeds, whether toasted or not, are a traditional ingredient in many Italian sausages and pasta sauces.

Parsnips

Parsnips are a root vegetable resembling white carrots, but not as uniform in thickness. It's a cold weather lover and grows bigger and more flavorful the further north it is planted. The longer they stay in the cold ground the more time they have to convert their starch into natural sugar. Commercial farmers use refrigerators. Keep Parsnips in there too. Parsnips have a sweet herbal flavor (sort of like a cross between a carrot, turnip and celeriac), which really comes out when they caramelize. Try to buy parsnips of uniform thickness since the ends can get woody if they are really thick. The thinner parsnips are sweeter and less pungent. They are a high fiber vegetable and rich in B vitamins, iron and folate.

Parsnips can be boiled but are wonderful roasted along with carrots or potatoes and make fantastic purees. Pairing cinnamon with the parsnips makes them sweet and hides the fact that they are white. Adding something like cider imparts notes of fruit. It is not cloyingly so, but offers just a hint of sweetness with the spice of cinnamon, making this seem like a dessert rather than a vegetable. Kids will be much inclined to try a piece. And getting them to try anything is the big hurdle. Also don't pick wild parsnips with your kids; there is a poisonous species of water hemlock out there that looks just like a parsnip.

Tortilla & Wraps

Wraps have become very popular for sandwiches transcending its traditional use as an old fashion burrito shell. Because of this popularity, here is some interesting information. We have a few recipes in this book using wraps. Wraps are generally made with Flour, Corn or Wheat.

Corn Tortillas:

The Mayans and the Aztecs made their tortillas by soaking corn kernels in a lime/water solution to remove the skin and then grinded them into dough (called 'Masa'). Then it is rolled in a ball, pounded flat and cooked on a hot griddle. It was an amazingly healthy dietary staple and a large part of both cultures. You can find corn tortillas made this way in stores, albeit with a tortilla press and assembly line. The list of ingredients is what's important, especially if you have dietary concerns. There are organic tortillas on the market. And some mass-market brands are quite good too. Sometimes you will see the word "sprouted" on the label. Sprouting activates enzymes from the whole kernel making it a nutrient rich food. This process naturally increases the protein content, while decreasing the calories and carbohydrates found in the original grain. Tortillas made from corn flour, while still healthful, are not sprouted. Once again, it comes down to reading the ingredient list—which should be as short as possible.

Look for whole grain tortillas, made with water and lime and as few long words in the ingredient list as possible!

Note About Tortilla Wraps: An 8 inch flour tortilla has about 150 calories, a little more than a single slice of bread. Of course, a sandwich usually uses two slices of bread, so you are getting a few less calories with a wrap. I mention this because wraps are not as low cal as people think. If you eat two or three wraps at a seating, you are taking in quite a bit of calories. This is a concern if weight is an issue for you or your kids. An 8 inch whole wheat tortilla wrap has about a 95 calories and an 8 inch corn tortilla wrap has around 50. (Amounts will vary depending on the brand your purchase. Again these are close approximations). Protein content for an 8 inch flour tortilla is around 4 grams, and it descends from there with whole wheat providing 3.3 grams and corn providing 2.5 grams. Corn tortillas are also gluten free.

Quick Tips for Cooking Meat

These Rules Hold True whether you are Frying, Searing, Braising or even Grilling.

Cook It at Room Temperature.

The meat will release too much moisture while it comes up to temperature as you cook it. You will have problems in the browning and in sticking to the pan. The oil should shimmer in the pan before you add the cut of meat (for that matter vegetables too). You won't get sick if you leave the meat on the counter for an hour.

Get Your Pan Blazing Hot.

Then turn to medium low once you've attained a sear on the meat. The sear keeps the flavor and juice in the meat and adds taste.

Stainless Steel and Cast Iron Cookware.

Invest in a heavy bottomed, stainless steel piece or cast iron. These are the best for fry pans, braisers, and Dutch ovens. Anything that needs to take heat. You won't have to replace it every few years and worry about whether or not PFOA is a real concern.

Use the Right Size Pan.

Never, ever over crowd what you are cooking.

Let the Meat Rest.

This is critical. Everyone warns against cutting the meat too soon and everyone is guilty of doing it from time to time. It makes a mess and all the flavor runs out on the cutting board and on your counter. There is carryover cooking time to consider. And this is the perfect opportunity to make pan sauce or gravy from the drippings left in the pan.

Chapter 6
Breakfast

Apple Orchard French Toast

I created this recipe during the fall, when I had an abundance of apples and was trying to come up with new ways to use them. It's super delicious and you won't be scrambling around the kitchen to prepare this weekend breakfast treat that both you and your children will enjoy together.

Ingredients:
- 1 Loaf Challah Bread, sliced 1 inch thick (make 2 slices per person)
- 1 Granny Smith Apple, sliced very thin
- 1 Apple (your favorite) sliced thin
- 4 Tbs. Cinnamon, divided in half
- 4 Large Eggs
- ½ Cup Milk
- ½ tsp. Nutmeg
- 1/4 Tsp. Cloves
- 1 Tbs. Vanilla
- 2 Tbs. Unsalted Butter

Procedure:
1. Pre Heat Oven to 200 F degrees
2. Make a pocket in each 1" thick slice of the Challah, by slicing through the center, but not slicing completely in half. Coat the Apple slices in a bowl with the sugar and 2 Tbsp Cinnamon. Place 2-3 Apple slices into each Challah pocket
3. In a shallow bowl or pan mix together eggs, milk, remaining 2 Tbsp Cinnamon, nutmeg, cloves, and vanilla, lightly beat.
4. Preheat a Non Stick Griddle or fry pan with 1 Tbsp Butter on medium-low
5. Dip Challah and apples sandwiches in egg mixture coating both sides of the sandwich, and one at a time place into or on to the Fry pan or griddle, cook until golden brown on both sides about 3-4 minutes per side. Place each piece of French Toast onto a heat proof plate and place in the oven until all Challah sandwiches are done
6. Take another apple, and slice it thin, dip the slices into the cinnamon sugar and place in the same non stick fry pan or griddle that you used for the Challah, allow to caramelize on medium-low heat on both sides.
7. To serve pull Challah out of the warm oven, place 2 slices onto a plate, add caramelized apples in between the 2 slices and serve with maple syrup.

Servings: 4. Preparation Time: 10 minutes. Cooking Time: 10 minutes.

Recipe Tips
Feel free to substitute any fruit you may like if apples are not your thing, Pears would be lovely in this breakfast sandwich. The options are limitless.

Family Notes

Banana Nut Banana Sandwiches

I love these pancake sandwiches: they are really easy. You can make up the pancakes days in advance and store them in between parchment paper in a zip lock bag at room temp, or freeze them, either way it is great to have on hand when your kids are hungry for a snack or bring friends home unexpectedly. Just slice up some Bananas, sprinkle with cinnamon sugar and sandwich between two pancakes. You and your kids will absolutely adore making and eating this quick little breakfast meal.

Ingredients:
- 1 Cup 100% Whole Wheat Flour
- 3 Tbs. White Sugar
- 1 Tsp. Baking Powder
- ½ Tsp. Baking Soda,
- 1/8 Tsp. Salt
- ½ Tsp Nutmeg
- 1 Tsp. Cinnamon
- ¼ Tsp. Cloves
- 1 Egg White
- 1 Cup Buttermilk
- 2 Tbs. Vegetable Oil
- 1 Tsp. Vanilla
- ½ Cup Walnuts, finely chopped
- 1 banana, sliced on a diagonal
- Butter or Cooking Spray

Procedure
1. Preheat either a non stick griddle or a Non stick 12 inch Fry Pan over medium heat.
2. In a large bowl combine all dry ingredients, set aside.
3. In a small bowl or 2 cup measuring glass combine, egg white, Vegetable Oil, and Vanilla.
4. Add all at once the liquid ingredients to the dry ingredients, using a silicone spatula mix to moisten, leave lumpy. Fold in Mashed Banana, and nuts.
5. Add 1 Tbsp of butter, or spray cooking surface, and begin to make small pancakes.
6. You should get about 12 pancakes out of this recipe, so 6 sandwiches.
7. Once the pancakes are done, take the sliced banana and dip them into the cinnamon sugar, then arrange 2 slices per pancake and top with remaining pancake.

Servings: 12. Preparation Time: 10 minutes. Cooking Time: 15 minutes.

Family Notes

Banana Oat Muffins with Mascarpone Frosting

A popular national donut shop chain sells pumpkin, blueberry, etc. muffins, which contain about 650 calories and twice the amount of fat found in a bacon & cheese egg muffin. Poor Nutritional qualities alone should prompt you to make your own muffins, and when you add in the cost of one of their muffins, you can make a batch of these.

Ingredients:
- 1 Cup All- Purpose Flour (always use unbleached you don't need the chemicals)
- 2 Cups Whole Wheat Pastry Flour
- 1 Tsp. Each : Baking Soda, Baking Powder, Salt, Ground Cinnamon
- ¼ Tsp. Each: Ground Nutmeg and All Spice
- ½ Cup Quick Cooking Oats (organic if you have it)
- 1 Cup Splenda or Florida Crystals (organic Sugar)
- 1 Cup Light Brown Sugar
- 1 Cup Vegetable Oil
- 3 Lg. Eggs
- 2 Tsp. Real Vanilla (again you don't need the chemicals)
- 4 Bananas, very ripe and coarsely mashed
- **Frosting:**
- 4 Tbsp. Unsalted Butter (at room temp.)
- 8 oz. Mascarpone Cheese (at room temp.), or cream cheese as a substitute.
- ¼ - 1/3 Cup Local Honey

Procedure:
1. You will need two bowls; one for wet and one for dry ingredients. Combine the flours and spices in a large bowl. I recommend using the Whole Wheat pastry flour with 1 cup A.P. flour because the pastry flour makes a lighter muffin. There are additional nutrition benefits with the Whole Wheat flour too.

2. Combine the sugars and wet ingredients in medium sized bowl. (It is OK to substitute 2 cups of white sugar if you do not have Splenda or Florida crystals or light brown sugar.)

3. Combine the wet ingredients into the large bowl. Fold in well.

4. Then fill each cup with batter. You can use the traditional metal muffin tin, which will need to be coated with butter or sprayed with a non-stick spray, or use silicone muffin cups (which I really love because they clean up effortlessly and require no spray).

5. Bake for 25 – 30 minutes in a 325 F degree oven.

Frosting:
1. Mix all three ingredients together and pipe or spread onto cooled muffins. That's it!

Servings: 18. Preparation Time: 15 minutes. Cooking Time: 30 minutes.

Family Notes

Blueberry Lime Cream Cheese Spread

Wow, think how cool and what a unique flavor blueberries and limes have when combined in a spread. It becomes really pretty as the blueberries break up and spread their beautiful colors of navy blue and deep reddish purple throughout the cream cheese. The lime zest's bright chartreuse color really pops against the blues and purples. And blueberries and limes are loaded with vitamins and antioxidants making them a "super food".

Ingredients:
- 8 oz. Reduced Fat Cream Cheese
- 4 Slices Whole Wheat Toast or Bagels
- ¼ Cup Blueberry preserve, or fruit preserve to your liking
- 1 Lime, zested

Procedure
1. Mix all ingredients together and serve. That's really all there is to it. It couldn't be simpler and the kids can do it pretty much alone.

Servings: 4. Preparation Time: 5 minutes.

Recipe Tips
Blueberries have the highest anti-oxidant capacity of any fresh fruit. Antioxidants like Vitamins A, B complex, C, E, Anthocyanin (responsible for the blue color), copper, selenium, and zinc help boost your immune system. They are also believed to stave off age related health conditions. Blueberries are also high in fiber. According to the FDA, one serving of blueberries (1 Cup / 140 grams) meets 50% of recommended daily allowance of fruit. A ½ cup is good for Kids.

Limes are another fruit rich in anti-oxidants and have been used for centuries because of their taste and health benefits. The entire British Navy carried limes aboard ship to fight disease for over 200 years. .

Family Notes

Eggs Foo Young

As I sat in my parent's living room one Sunday Morning mulling over breakfast recipes for this cookbook, the familiar smell of eggs and bacon came wafting in as my father prepared his Sunday breakfast. It brought back memories of being little and spending my summers up in Vermont with my family. My Father was always the first one up, and therefore the maker of breakfast. Vermont mornings even in the summer are a bit cool and it's hard to get out of a snuggly bed. I would wake up to the smell of eggs and bacon, and bundle up in sweat pants and a sweat shirt and run down stairs to my Dad. The Kitchen door would be closed and my Dad had to use this ancient electric heater we had to get the kitchen nice and warm. When I opened that creaky door I was immediately hit with the warmth and the smell of yummy food. My Dad would make me a concoction he called "Eggs Foo Young". To this day I still love this breakfast, as I know you and your child will.

Ingredients:
- 4 Whole Wheat English Muffins, toasted and buttered
- 4 Sunny Side Down Cooked Eggs, middles still runny
- 8 Pieces of Bacon, cooked
- Salt and Pepper to taste
- Paprika, to taste, if desired

Procedure
1. Toast each English Muffin, and butter each side

2. Cook your eggs in a large non stick fry pan, sunny side down, but don't overcook the eggs ~ there needs to be some uncooked yolk. Sprinkle salt, pepper, and paprika on both sides of the eggs.

3. Fry up 8 pieces of Bacon, drain on a plate lined with paper towels

4. To Assemble: place 1 half of an English Muffin in the bottom of a bowl, top with 2 pieces of bacon and 1 egg, top with other half of English muffin, then with a knife and fork cut it all up together mixing the muffin, bacon, and egg (this is why you want a soft egg center, because when you cut it all up it coats everything and makes it that much more yummy)

5. To increase the flavor put a pinch of Paprika on each egg along with sea salt and fresh ground pepper. This last unexpected bit of spice adds a flourish of color, tasty zest and brightens any morning. If you are concerned about salt intake-just use the paprika it's a great way to eliminate salt but not flavor.

Servings: 4. Preparation Time: 5 minutes. Cooking Time: 10 minutes.

Family Notes

Energy Burrito

This is so simple and yet packed with so much energy to keep you and your child on the move all morning. Another quick breakfast or mid-day snack recipe your kids can make for themselves.

Ingredients;
- Whole Wheat Wrap
- 1 Banana, peeled and sliced
- 1 Apple (of your liking) sliced thin
- 1 Tbsp Reduced Fat Peanut Butter
- 1 Tbsp Local Honey
- ¼ Tsp. Flaxseed

Procedure
1. Spread the peanut butter onto the center of the wrap
2. Add your slices of banana and apple
3. Drizzle with the honey, and sprinkle with flaxseed
4. Roll bottom of wrap up first, then bring in the sides, you can microwave this for 10-15 seconds for a warm breakfast or just wrap and go.

Servings: 1. Preparation Time: 5 minutes.

Family Notes

Izzy's Favorite Breakfast Roll-up

My friend Cheryl Velasquez has a teenage daughter who came up this recipe. It's an easy enough recipe for Isabella to make before leaving for school. Isabella has helped us out with promotional events too. Cheryl and Isabella thank you for sharing this recipe.

Ingredients:
- 2 Eggs, beaten
- 1 –2 slices of American Cheese
- 2 Slices Bacon, cooked (optional)
- 1 Tbsp. Butter or Olive Oil
- 1 Flour Tortilla Shell (10 inch round)

Procedure
1. Heat the butter or olive oil in a small skillet until hot*. (Butter will brown and begin to bubble, oil will shimmer in the pan.) Add the eggs and scramble until done. Place the cheese slices on top of the eggs and just as they start to melt remove from heat. Cover with a lid (or a plate) for 2 to 3 minutes. The cheese will continue to melt but the eggs won't overcook.

2. Place a tortilla on a plate and put the cheesy eggs across the middle. Top with the crispy bacon. Roll up the bottom and top of the tortilla first, then fold over the sides, and turn upside down. Cover with a paper towel and microwave for approximately 8 – 10 seconds to soften the tortilla shell and make sure it sticks together. (Every microwave is different so your time will vary). Eat carefully; it could be very hot inside. I like to poke the tortilla with a fork in several locations to let potential steam out.

3. Tortilla shells are made from a variety of ingredients, corn, flour, wheat, 100% whole wheat and some have added vegetables in the mix like spinach or sun-dried tomato. For people with dietary issues, tortillas do offer options. For example: corn tortillas tend to be gluten free (read the manufacturers label to be sure) and are good for people who can't ingest wheat.

* A last note: if you are cooking bacon for this tortilla, use the same pan to cook the eggs. You won't need to use any butter or oil. Even after you drain off the grease, there will be enough residual bacon fat to keep the eggs from sticking and a lot of flavor!.

Servings: 1. Preparation Time: 5 minutes. Cooking Time: Less than 5 minutes.

Family Notes

Pumpkin Chocolate Chip Muffins

Here is another excellent muffin that won't supply you and your kids with a whole days worth of sugar and calories. This requires little effort and the pumpkin and chocolate combination is uncommonly delectable. I'm recommending you blend in a cup of whole-wheat pastry flour (with the AP flour) if you can. The Pastry flour makes a lighter and airy muffin and there is a nutritional benefit to 100% whole-wheat flour. Cutting back on the butter with some plain yogurt reduces the fat content and adds a source of extra calcium and protein.

Ingredients:

- 1 2/3 Cups Unbleached All Purpose Flour (I use Whole Wheat Pastry flour)
- 2/3 Cups Sugar
- Nutmeg, Cinnamon, Clove (¼ tsp each) or 1 Tbsp Pumpkin Pie Spice.
- 1 Tbsp Baking Soda
- ¼ Tsp. Baking Powder
- ¼ Tsp Salt
- 2 Large Eggs
- 1 Cup Plain Pumpkin Puree
- ½ Cup Melted Butter (I like using a ¼ cup butter and a ¼ cup yogurt or oil)
- 1 ½ - 2 Cups Chocolate Chips (depending on how chocolaty you like it)

Procedure

1. Heat your oven to 350 degrees F.

2. Thoroughly mix your dry ingredients (flour, sugar, pie spice, salt, baking powder and soda) in a large bowl. Break your eggs in a second bowl. It's easier than looking for shells in your dry mix. Add the pumpkin and the butter (or yogurt) to the eggs and whisk until well blended. Stir in the chocolate chips.

3. Pour the wet mixture over the dry ingredients and fold in with a rubber spatula just until everything is moistened. Again do not over work the batter. Scoop the batter into baking cups.

4. Bake 20 –25 minutes. You'll know they are done when the muffins will be puffed and springy to the touch (a tooth pick will come out clean). Turn out on a rack to cool.

Servings: 18. Preparation Time: 15 minutes. Cooking Time: 25 minutes.

Family Notes

Strawberries & Cream Cheese
Breakfast Sandwiches

I like using Challah bread for this recipe because it is hearty enough to stand up to the strawberries, yet is still sweet and delicate to the palate. It fries well and kids like it. You will have many uses for the entire loaf.

Ingredients: (makes 4 sandwiches)
- 1 Cup Reduced Fat Cream Cheese
- 8 Slices of Challah Bread (sliced 1/2 inch thick)
- 1 Pint Fresh Strawberries, sliced as evenly as possible
- 1 Egg
- ¾ Cup 2% Milk
- 1 Tbsp. Vanilla Extract
- ½ Tsp. Cinnamon
- ¼ Tsp Nutmeg
- ¼ Cup Confectioner's Sugar
- Cooking Spray, Butter flavored if you have it.

Procedure
1. Set out 4 of the slices of Challah bread and top each slice with about a 1/4 of the cream cheese. Then lay on the sliced strawberries and top with the remaining 4 slices of bread. Gently press together.

2. In a shallow dish combine the milk, egg, cinnamon, nutmeg and vanilla. Then coat a frying pan with cooking spray and heat to medium. You can coat your first sandwich while you are waiting, but do not coat all of them. You don't want them to become soggy.

3. Dip each sandwich into the milk mixture and flip to get both sides coated. Then set in the frying pan. Cook for about 3 –4 minutes per side. Dust with powdered sugar and set on a tray. Dip and Cook remaining sandwiches and serve.

Servings: 4. Preparation Time: 15 minutes. Cooking Time: 10 minutes.

Family Notes

Strawberry Mint Breakfast Parfait

Let's face it breakfast can sometimes be the hardest meal to get into ourselves let alone our kids. Mornings are busy. You know this is especially true on school days. So this healthy parfait can be made the night before, placed into the fridge and pulled out in the morning to be eaten before racing off.

Again we are using local honey. Local honey is important for many reasons. Buying local supports your community and the local environment and offers possible immunity boosters for you and your family's health. Bees and pollination are important across the globe. Local honey producers should be supported in the region you live in because of the benefits bees bring are seen regionally.

Raw Honey: If you can find local raw honey, try it. Raw honey has a different consistency, its' not a liquid translucent amber, it is creamy, cloudy and yellowy. Raw honey is minimally filtered has not been heated like the familiar liquid honeys, and thereby retains its beneficial enzymes and nutrients. Raw honey offers you another talking point to educate kids about the importance of bees and local farming

Ingredients:
- A Pint Strawberries, washed
- 1 Lime, Juiced
- 1 Tbsp. Local Honey
- Fresh Mint, leaves finely chopped
- 4 Containers of Vanilla Greek Yogurt (8 oz. each)

Procedure
1. Wash, remove the stems of the strawberries and slice.
2. In a bowl combine the Strawberries, honey, lime juice, and mint- let sit for 15 minutes or overnight.

Serve in a container of your choice, layering the fruit and yogurt.

Servings: 4. Preparation Time: 10 minutes. Inactive Time: 15 minutes.

Family Notes

Super-Hero Muffins

These Muffins are wonderful for many reasons. The kids love them because all they taste are the chocolate chips. Even the pickiest children will delight in eating them. The list of ingredients might seem long, but it is necessary for the overall nutritional benefit. We are using Whole Wheat Pastry Flour because it produces a much less dense muffin. You can also mix your chocolate chips half and half with dark chocolate and semi- sweet chips because of dark chocolate's level of anti-oxidants and health benefits. The shredded Apples and Carrots really go a long way to keep the muffins sweet and moist, even after freezing. Carrots are known for improving vision and blood sugar and beneficial to heart and lung and colon health. Apples are very good source of antioxidants, fiber and flavoniods. They have a positive effect on the body's cholesterol levels, and aid with digestion. One large apple provides about 30% of the fiber that should be consumed daily.

I hope you try these Super-Hero muffins really soon. Your kids will love them. These can be made up ahead of time and freeze really well. Also, Raisins can be substituted for the Chocolate Chips if sugar content is an issue. Use Yellow Raisins and soak them over night in apple juice to soften and reduce the raisin's structure. It will make the raisins more palatable to children. Don't be put off by the relatively extensive ingredient list. Keep in mind once you have all the ingredients on hand, you can make batches and batches of these super muffins. They become cost effective in the long run.

Ingredients:
- 1 Cup Whole Wheat Pastry Flour
- ½ Cup Unbleached Flour
- 1 Cup Flaxseed Meal
- ½ Cup Oat Bran
- 1 Cup Packed Brown Sugar
- 2 Tsp Baking Soda
- 1 Tsp Baking Powder
- ½ Tsp Salt
- 2 Tsp Cinnamon
- ½ Tsp Nutmeg
- ¼ Tsp Ground Cloves
- 2 Cups Finely Shredded Carrots
- 2 Peeled and Shredded Apples
- 1 -1½ Cups Chocolate Chips
- ¾ Cup Fat Free Milk
- 2 Eggs, Beaten
- 1 Tsp Real Vanilla

Procedure
1. Preheat Oven to 350 F degrees. Combine all Dry ingredients in a large bowl. Then Add Carrots, Apples, and Chocolate Chips to dry ingredients, toss lightly, coating the carrots, apples and chips.
2. Combine in a small bowl, Milk, Eggs, and Vanilla, Whisk to Combine.
3. Add Liquid ingredients to dry, and mix till just moist. DO NOT OVER MIX.
4. Using a muffin scoop, fill your muffin tins ½ full.
5. Bake for 15-20 minutes.

Servings: 24. Preparation Time: 20 minutes. Cooking Time: 25 minutes.

Family Notes

Chapter 7
Lunch

Carrot Salad

It is all about being creative and quick when it comes to lunches, especially if your child brings a lunch to school. This recipe could not be any simpler, or more delicious.

Ingredients:
- Grated Carrots, About 1 Cup
- 1 Small Can of Pineapple chunks (drained, reserve the juice)
- ½ Cup Dried cranberries
- ¼ Cup Walnuts
- 8 oz. Vanilla Greek Yogurt
- ¼ Cup Pineapple Juice
- 1 Tbsp Local Honey
- Zest of 1 Orange

Procedure
1. for Salad: combine the carrots, pineapple, cranberries, and nuts set aside
2. For the Dressing: Combine the yogurt, pineapple juice, orange zest, and honey mix to combine.
3. Pour dressing over salad, toss to combine, and either serve or put in refrigerator for 30 minutes up to overnight.

Servings: 1. Degree of Difficulty: Very Easy.

Preparation Time: 10 minutes. Total Time: 10 minutes.

Recipe Tips
The longer the dressing is allowed to meld with the salad ingredients the better the taste will be. This is great for school lunches, and easy to make the night before.

Family Notes

Great Grilled Cheese

The last time I was in Chicago, I had this excellent grilled cheese sandwich on pumpernickel bread for lunch at a place called Hot Chocolate. (It was winter and brutally cold. And, of course, they served this unbelievably good hot chocolate drink too.) This is my take on that sandwich. It has raw honey, cheddar cheese, and slices of apple all between slices of pumpernickel bread.

Pumpernickel is an aromatic, dark rye bread with a very thin crust and something akin to a sweet dark chocolate coffee taste. The true German style is rye based and uses a sourdough starter. It becomes dark by a Maillard reaction (a non-enzymatic browning caused by amino acids and reducing sugars via heat). No coloring agents are used. Pumpernickel is baked very, very slowly at a low temperature in a steam filled oven. You can find German Style pumpernickel in specialty bakeries. The taste is much better than the mass-produced loaves that use molasses or cocoa to darken the blend of wheat and rye flours. Most American style pumpernickels are made with wheat and rye grains and really are just darkened rye bread. Many times the bakeries will add a lot of caraway seeds which changes the taste. It's worth the effort to look for the authentic stuff. True German style pumpernickel has a Low Glycemic Index, high fiber content and acts as a digestive aid because it breaks down in the colon due to its resistant starch content.

Ingredients (1 sandwich)
- 2 Slices Pumpernickel Bread
- 1 Granny Smith Apple, thinly sliced enough to cover the slice of bread
- Aged Sharp Cheddar Cheese, enough to cover the bread
- Local Raw Honey, enough to cover both slices of bread

Procedure
1. Slice the bread and apple and cheese. Coat each slice of bread with a layer of local honey. (The honey obviously goes in the inside of the bread slice.) Then stack across the bread the sliced cheddar, followed on top by the Granny Smith apple. Cover them with the second piece of pumpernickel. Grill in a preheated skillet or sauté pan. Cook for 2 –3 minutes per side, or until you see the cheese starting the melt out from the edges. You can also heat this sandwich in a conventional or toaster oven until the cheese has melted.

2. See, -- its as easy as making a grilled cheese sandwich!

Servings: 1. Preparation Time: 5 minutes. Cooking Time: 10 minutes.

Source: Hot Chocolate in Chicago

Family Notes

Grilled Apple & Cheese (Gluten- Free)

Another way to enjoy this little sandwich is without the bread. You are curious to try this now, aren't you?

Ingredients:
- 3 –4 Granny Smith Apples, sliced into a even flat pieces
- ¼ Cup Locally Produced Honey
- ¼ lb. Aged Cheddar (or your favorite brand) sliced evenly

Procedure
1. Slice the Granny Smith Apples fairly thick into even slices. Discard the seeds and core. Have a baking sheet ready to set these little apple sandwiches upon. Coat the apple slices with local honey. I like using a small silicone brush to spread the honey. The honey spreads better and the silicone is more flexible and cleaner than the old fashion bristle brushes. Layer with cheddar cheese slices, sticking them onto the honey coated apple. Top with a second piece of apple, making a small sandwich. Then bake in a conventional or toaster oven set at 300 F. Bake until cheese begins to melt out from between the apple slices.

Servings: 4. Preparation Time: 5 minutes. Cooking Time: 5 minutes.

Recipe Tips
The tartness of the Granny Smith Apple is a classic combination with Aged Cheddar and the sweetness of honey. This is easy enough for kids to make pretty much all by themselves. A very healthy little snack, especially if you need to eat Gluten Free and crave a 'grilled cheese sandwich'.

It's also a unique party hors d' oeuvre for people of any age. Kids might prefer American Cheddar but you can experiment with a variety of aged cheddars for the adults.

Family Notes

Protein Packed Pita Pockets
(White Bean Dip with Pita Chips)

This takes minutes to make and packs all the power of the mighty legume. It is so very good --you won't want to buy bean dip from a store anymore. Plus by making it yourself you can regulate the ingredients and how much salt is used. Look for a pita pocket made with whole grains. Read the label, the dietary content varies greatly by brand.

Ingredients:
- 1 (15oz.) Can Cannellini Beans, drained and rinsed
- 2 Cloves Garlic
- 2 Tbsp. Fresh Lemon juice and zest of same lemon
- 1/3-Cup Olive Oil, plus 4 Tbsp. (best quality --its important)
- ¼ Cup Fresh Italian Parsley
- Salt & Pepper
- 6 Pitas
- 1 Tsp. Herbs: Oregano or Basil or Thyme. Blended Italian Herb Mix works well too.

Procedure
1. Preheat oven to 400 F degrees. Using a food processor put the beans, garlic, lemon juice and 1/3 cup of olive oil in the bowl and pulse until the mixture is coarsely chopped into a puree. Don't over work the ingredients. Season with salt and pepper to taste and transfer the puree into a small bowl.

2. For the Pitas, cut each in half and then into even wedges. You should get 8 wedges from each pita. Lightly drizzle on some olive oil –just enough so that the salt and pepper and herbs will stick when you sprinkle them on top of the wedges. Bake for 8 – 12 minutes. Serve at room temperature alongside the bowl of puree.

Servings: 6. Preparation Time: 8 minutes. Cooking Time: 12 minutes.

Family Notes

Spicy Roast Beef Wrap

This is an excellent roast beef wrap, spicy and easy to assemble. There is a clean bright heat from the green chilies combined with a sweet tanginess from the Russian dressing that coats the meat. It's a great way to use up that left over Sunday roast.

Ingredients:
- 6 Thinly sliced pieces of Roast Beef
- 2 Pieces of Good Cheddar Cheese
- 2 Tbsp. Canned Green Chilies, chopped
- 2 Tbsp. Russian Dressing

Procedure
1. Lay out your wrap, spread the Russian dressing onto the center of the wrap, place the Roast Beef, Cheddar, and Chilies on top, then wrap up, either by rolling the ends or folding in all four sides to make a package.

2. You could microwave this wrap for 10-15 seconds to melt the cheese, or you could stick it on a grill pan and warm it up, then let it cool, wrap in foil and off to school it goes.

Servings: 1. Preparation Time: 5 minutes.

Family Notes

Roasted Vegetable Wrap with Herb Spread

Ingredients:
- 1 small Eggplant, peeled, and sliced into ½" thick slices, length wise
- 1 Red Pepper, cut in to thick sliced
- 1 Yellow Pepper, cut in to thick slices
- 1 Yellow or Red Onion, peeled and sliced into ½" thick slices
- 1 Zucchini, sliced into ½" pieces length wise
- 6oz. Mushrooms, sliced
- 2 - 3 Tablespoons Extra Virgin Olive Oil
- Course Kosher Salt
- Fresh Black Pepper

Herb Spread:
- 8oz. Reduced Fat Cream Cheese, room temperature
- 2-3 Tablespoons Milk
- 1 Tablespoon (each) of Fresh Thyme, Oregano, Mint, Parsley or any herbs you like. If you do not have fresh herbs available use 1 **Teaspoon** each of dried herbs of your choice
- Kosher Salt
- Fresh Black Pepper
- 4 Large Soft Whole Wheat Wraps

Procedure:
1. Preheat oven to 375 F degrees

2. On a cookie sheet place all you sliced vegetables, coat with olive oil, salt and pepper.

3. Roast for 30 to 45 minutes, or until soft and carmelized.

4. Meanwhile place cream cheese into a small bowl, add enough milk to thin. You want a consistency of yogurt. Add in your herbs and mix well to combine.

5. Remove vegetables from the oven when done, and allow to cool 10 to 15 minutes

6. Spread each wrap with the herb cheese spread, top with roasted vegetables, wrap and serve, or wrap tightly in plastic wrap and place in refrigerator.

Family Notes

The Inside-Out Sandwich

Ingredients:

- Boston or Bibb lettuce
- ½ lb. Deli Meat of your choosing, sliced thin
- ½ cup Reduced Fat Cream Cheese, room temperature
- 1 Carrot, peeled and using a peeler, peel into long thin strips of carrot
- Sandwich Pickles, brand of your choice, they must be the long flat sandwich pickles
- Soft Bread Sticks or Sub Rolls (about 6 to 8 inches long)

Procedure:

1. Lay out 1 to 2 pieces of lettuce (you want the lettuce to be about the same length as the bread stick), place a few slices of deli meat on top of the lettuce.

2. Spread 1 to 2 tablespoons of cream cheese on top of the meat.

3. Lay a few strips of carrot over the cream cheese, and then lay a pickle over the carrot.

4. Place the bread stick at the longest edge of the lettuce, and slowly roll the lettuce/meat around the bread stick.

5. You should now have the bread stick in the center, and the lettuce on the exterior.

6. Wrap each sandwich tight in plastic wrap, and refrigerate for at least 30 minutes, preferably over night.

Family Notes

Hummus Garden Sandwich

Simplicity in a sandwich is a good thing and when the same sandwich offers an array of fresh vegetables and a proper protein to carbohydrate ratio it's a great thing. Your body needs carbs and proteins to energize you through the afternoon. This sandwich can be altered in so many ways by just changing the variety of vegetables by season or that your family favors. So you can create this sandwich over and over and never get tired of it. Try different flavored Hummus's to jazz things up. It makes a great lunch box item, especially since there is no mayonnaise to spoil.

Ingredients:
- 8oz. prepared Hummus, flavor and brand of your choice
- 4 Whole Wheat Sandwich buns
- 1 Small Head of Boston Lettuce, or any soft lettuce you can find
- 2 Tomatoes, sliced about ¼" to ½" thick
- 1 Cucumber, sliced thin
- 1 Carrot, peeled into thin strips using a vegetable peeler, run the length of the carrot
- 1 Red Onion, sliced thin (optional)

Procedure:
1. 1. Separate tops and bottoms of bread.
2. 2. Spread 2 to 3 tablespoons of hummus on both top and bottom of bread.
3. 3. Add remaining ingredients to bottom halves of buns and top with top bun.

Recipe Tip
The main ingredients in Hummus are chick peas, tahini (a sesame seed paste) and olive oil. It is high in iron, monounsaturated fats, Vitamins C and B6, folate, dietary fiber, and protein. The amino acid profile in tahini nutritionally complements the chick peas. Hummus digests best when eaten with fresh vegetables. Combined with whole grains, hummus proves a complete protein. Maybe that's why it's been around for more than 5000 years.

Family Notes

Pizza Tortilla Sandwich

This "Pizza" style tortilla can be made with any vegetable you and your children like. It can also be made ahead of time, cooled, and stored in wedges in a zip lock bag inside the refrigerator. Use it for a lunch box item, or with a quick microwaving you'll have a snack for them when they get home.

Ingredients:
- 8 Soft Corn or Whole Wheat Tortillas
- 1 Can of Diced Tomatoes, any brand you like (15 oz. can)
- 8oz. Shredded Mozzarella (usually available in 8 oz. bags)
- 8oz. Shredded Cheddar, or cheese of your liking
- 1 Red, Yellow, or Green Pepper, diced small
- 1 container of Sliced Mushrooms (about 6 oz.)
- 1 Bag of pre-sliced Pepperoni, (for a meatless version add a can of your favorite beans; black, kidney, cannellini)
- 1 tablespoon Dried Italian Seasoning
- 2 tablespoons Olive Oil
- Sea Salt

Procedure:
1. Preheat oven 350 F.

2. Lay out the 4 tortillas onto a cookie sheet, spread 4 pieces with the canned diced tomato, top with mozzarella, and cheddar, top cheese with peppers, mushrooms, and pepperoni. Sprinkle Italian seasoning over top of vegetable. Top with the other 4 tortillas.

3. Using a small pastry brush, brush tops of tortilla pizzas with a little olive oil, then sprinkle with salt (if using).

4. Bake in oven for 5-10 minutes or until the cheese has melted and the tortilla's have fused together.

5. Allow to cool for a few minutes, before slicing and serving.

Family Notes

Quinoa Spiced Dried Fruit Medley

Quinoa is very good made either sweet or savory. This recipe uses both taste sensations.

Ingredients:
- 1 Cup Quinoa
- 1 cup assorted Dried Fruit, diced small
- 2 ¼ Cups Water
- ½ cup Yellow Raisins
- 1 Tablespoon Cumin
- 1 Tablespoon Cinnamon
- ¼ Teaspoon Chili Powder
- Kosher Salt, to taste
- Fresh Black Pepper, to taste
- ½ Cup Pepita's (shelled pumpkin seeds)

Procedure:
1. Bring the water up to a boil in a 2quart saucepan, add the quinoa, dried fruit, raisins, cumin, cinnamon, chili powder, salt, and pepper, mix to combine, bring back to a boil, cover and cook on medium heat for about 10-12 minutes, or until quinoa has absorbed all the water, remove from heat, fluff, and let stand for 15 minutes.

2. Top with Pepita's and serve, or allow to cool completely, place in an airtight container and refrigerate until ready to use.

Servings: 4. Preparation Time: 5 minutes.

Family Notes

Turkey-Bacon-Avocado Pita

Cranberry sauce is wonderful all year. It is inexpensive, good for you and really useful on sandwiches and a fine substitute for mayonnaise. More importantly, -- it will not spoil. The naturally occurring tannins in cranberry sauce can reduce the chances of bacterial growth. Combining cranberry sauces' tartness with the creaminess of an avocado and smokey flavor of turkey breast and crispy bacon makes a sandwich that is hard to become bored by.

Ingredients:
- 8oz. Whole Cranberry Sauce, any brand of your choosing
- 4 Whole Wheat Pita Pockets
- Avocado, peeled, and sliced
- 8 Slices of cooked Bacon, 2 per pocket
- ½ lb. Smoked Turkey Breast, sliced thin

Procedure:
1. Open up each pita pocket; spread the cranberry sauce on the inside of each pocket.
2. Place 2 slices of Avocado on either side on the interior of the pocket.
3. Place 2 slices of bacon on either side of the avocado.
4. Add the turkey in the center of it all, and serve or wrap and send it to school with the kids.

Family Notes

French Toast Banana Sandwich

Ingredients:

- 4 Thick Slices of French Toast (see recipe Below)
- 4oz. Reduced Fat Cream Cheese, room temperature
- 1 Banana, sliced thin
- Cinnamon, to taste
- 4oz. Nutella (Chocolate Hazelnut spread)

Procedure:

1. Spread cream cheese onto 2 of the 4 slices of French Toast
2. Place a layer of bananas over the cream cheese, and sprinkle with cinnamon.
3. Spread Nutella onto the other 2 pieces of French toast
4. Place the Nutella spread pieces on top of the banana's.

French Toast:

- 1 cup Milk
- 1 Egg, slightly beaten
- 1 tablespoon of Vanilla extract
- 1 tablespoon Cinnamon
- 1 teaspoon Nutmeg
- ¼ teaspoon Ground Cloves
- 1 loaf of Challah Bread, sliced into ½" thick slices

Procedure:

1. Combine all ingredients, except for the Challah, into a medium bowl, dip bread into milk mixture, and place into the fry pan, brown 3-5 minutes on each side.
2. Allow to cool completely.

These can be made the day before, cooled, and put into a zip lock bag, put into the refrigerator, until ready to use, or do a larger batch and freeze for up to 1 month.

Family Notes

Mango-Turkey Sub

The combination of the mango and cheese and apple, really makes this sandwich sing. The sweet and spicy mango chutney mixed in with the cool and creamy cream cheese, gives you this burst of flavor, while the Havarti cheese and apple follow with the surprise of harmony in your mouth. This sandwich to is another great lunch box item, and if the Mango chutney is not your favorite substitute it for your favorite jam.

Ingredients:
- ¼ cup Mango Chutney
- 8oz. Reduced Fat Cream Cheese
- Fresh ground Pepper
- 1 6" Sub roll, cut in half
- 1lb. Deli Turkey, sliced thin
- 4 Bibb Lettuce Leaves, or any variety of soft lettuce you like
- Reduced fat Havarti Cheese, sliced thin or any variety of cheese you desire
- 1 Medium Apple, of your liking, cored and sliced into rings

Procedure:
1. Combine the first 3 ingredients, spread on both sides of bread.
2. Top with lettuce, turkey, cheese, and apple.

Family Notes

Turkey and Cheese with Pesto Sandwich

Here's another one of Isabella Velasquez's recipes. This one makes a really good and fast lunch and has a proven popularity with teenagers. It uses simple ingredients most of which are always on hand.

Ingredients:
- 2 Slices Foccacia Bread (white or 100% Whole Wheat bread works too)
- 3-4 slices Turkey breast (thinly sliced from the deli)
- 1 Slice Mozzarella Cheese
- 3- Slices Tomato
- Real Mayonnaise
- Pesto (preferably Homemade)

Procedure
1. Set out the two slices of bread and lay the cheese slice upon one.

2. Spread the mayo and pesto on the cheese. This keeps the bread from becoming too soggy.

3. Top with the slices turkey and then the tomato. Cover with the second piece of bread and cut in half then enjoy.

How To Make Pesto:

Pesto is not as difficult to make as one would think. It is little more than fresh basil and good olive oil. In the summer, you should invest the time with your kids and plant fresh basil in the garden. A large planter or pot is also a great way to grow most herbs. You only need a sunny location and basil grows extremely well with very little care. One little plant at the garden center will cost you what one clump does at the grocery store. And that single plant will give you herbs all summer and fall. Oregano, thyme, and many other herbs are equally as bountiful. And Kids actually like planting and then harvesting the herbs. A great family activity—even in the city.

Combine Fresh Basil leaves, Olive Oil, ¼ cup of Pine Nuts with 1 or 2 Garlic Cloves in a blender or food processor. Pulse till smooth in consistency. You will need to keep drizzling in the oil as you go. Adding some grated Parmesan cheese doesn't hurt either – and the pine nuts can be omitted for allergy concerns.

Servings: 4. Preparation Time: 10 minutes.

Family Notes

Chapter 8
Dinner

Baked Spiced Corned Beef Brisket

You can bake your brisket instead of boiling it. Covered with mustard or a spice rub you can turn this into a versatile crowd pleaser for your family. A great way to keep the kids interested is by soliciting their input. You want a southwestern flair or a traditional brisket with garlic? Add some North African Spices (Moroccan spice mixes contain allspice berries, ground cayenne, cassia bark, cardamom, cut galangal, cinnamon, black pepper, ginger, lavender, turmeric and maybe many others. You can look for a pre-mixed blend at a good food store). The key is long, slow cooking. This is really not a 'once a year' dish. It's economical enough. I like to make this on the morning of a big game day. No one has complained whether they are watching football, baseball or basketball. It's a great main course and the sandwiches are wonderful!

Ingredients

- 1 Center-cut corned beef brisket (about 4 – 5 lbs.)
- 1 Lemon, thinly sliced
- 1 Onion peeled and thinly sliced
- 1 Tsp Black Peppercorns
- 1 –2 Cloves crushed Garlic
- 1/2 Tsp Allspice
- 6 to 8 Whole Cloves
- 1/4 Cup Dijon Mustard
- 1/4 Cup Brown Sugar
- Optional spices all ¼ tsp. or to your taste; Cumin, Cayenne, Cardamom

Procedure

1. Trim and discard most of the surface fat from brisket. Rinse meat well under cool running water, to release the salts used in the corning process. The slow cooking will break down the fat and cook right through the entire piece of meat.

2. Lay meat, fattiest side up, in a 2-inch-deep, 11x15 inch-roasting pan. Sprinkle with peppercorns, allspice, garlic, cloves and/or your choice of optional spices. The spice rub will take longer to infuse into the meat. (For you hardcore enthusiasts, another rub method is to heavily coat the meat with spices making a paste. You would need to do this a few days before cooking. Your kids will think it's pretty cool to watch the brisket shrink as it sits in the fridge.) Place the lemon and onion slices over seasoned meat. About half way through the cooking process, when much of the liquid has evaporated, re-coat the brisket with the spices, replace the lemon and onion with new, and return to the oven.

3. Set pan on middle rack in a 325° F degree heated oven. Pour about 8 cups boiling water around brisket, seal the pan with foil, and bake until meat is very tender when pierced, about 4 hours. Uncover and drain off all but about 1 cup of the liquid. Discard the lemon slices.

4. Mix the mustard and brown sugar and then spread evenly over meat. Broil about 8 inches from heat until the mustard mixture begins to brown, 3 to 5 minutes. Transfer the brisket to a platter. This is great served hot, warm, or cold. Remember to slice meat across the grain.

Servings: 6 – 8. Preparation Time: 15 minutes. Cooking Time: 4 hours.

Family Notes

Braised Corned Beef & Cabbage Dinner

There is no easier meal than the ubiquitous St. Patrick's Day dinner of Corned Beef and Cabbage. What we call corned beef and cabbage is also known as a 'boiled dinner'. This is probably why so many people do not like it and only make it because the St. Patrick's Day tradition and revelry demands doing so. Boiling the corned beef, cutting it incorrectly and cooking the life out of the cabbage and carrots are all guilty of turning a tasty and simple, low calorie meal into one that people claim is greasy and colorless and full of hunks of lifeless cabbage floating in it. So why not prepare the meat a little differently and cook the cabbage and vegetables separately and for the correct amount of time? I braise my beef brisket. The braising allows the meat's flavor to really come forth and avoids an over cooked, boiled mess. I mean, really, other for broth, would you boil a chicken?

Ingredients:
- 4-5 lbs Center Cut Beef Brisket (it will shrink by about half.)
- 1 Onion, cut in large pieces
- Water (or a couple bottles of Ale or Stout won't hurt. It's St. Patrick's Day.)
- 1 Savoy Cabbage, sliced
- 1 Lbs Carrots, chopped
- 2 Lbs White Potatoes, quartered (or Red if you like)
- 1 Small Handful or Black Peppercorns

Procedure
1. Rinse the brisket first. In a good cast iron Dutch oven with a tight fitting lid, heat some olive oil – enough to cover the bottom. Drop in your brisket and brown all the sides. (You may need to remove a little layer of the fat if it's very thick). Once browned, add enough liquid to almost cover the meat.

2. Add the chopped onion and the peppercorns. Put the lid on, turn down the heat, and simmer for 4 –5 hours. Just make sure the liquid does not completely evaporate during the cooking time. Braising, over low heat, will breakdown the connective tissues and melt the fat.

3. About a 45 minutes before the meat is done, add in your carrots. Boil the potatoes, in salted water, in a separate pot until soft (about 20 minutes). Drain. I like to get one of the kids to roughly smash them with a little butter and a splash or two of milk.

The Cabbage: Savoy is wonderful. It is prettier and has much more nuance than regular cabbage. Slice 1 head of Savoy cabbage into ribbons, while you heat olive oil and 2 pats of butter to a shimmer in a medium sauté pan. Toss about a quarter of the cabbage in the pan at a time as you sauté. It cooks fairly quickly.

Slice the meat across the grain and arrange on a platter with the cabbage, carrots and potatoes.

Serve with the mustard of your choice.

Servings: 12. (or 6 hungry people) Preparation Time: 10 minutes. Cooking Time: 4 to 5 hours.

Family Notes

Beef Shanks Beautifully Braised with Red Wine & Mushrooms

The aroma of this meal bubbling away in a bright Dutch Oven for 5 hours fills the house with everything I love about being home during the fall and winter or on a rainy spring day when the daffodils have just come out. It's a fantastic meal to make if you're away with your family and friends on a weekend ski trip (and worth the effort to lug the heavy pot with you!) Everyone will think you are a super chef. Don't tell them it's so very easy to make. I'm recommending 4 beef shanks, but you need to decide how much meat is on the shanks and how many people you need to feed. Ask the butcher for 'Soup Cut' and get a good look at each shank before you make your purchase. Feel free to increase the amount of beef, and add only a little extra seasoning to your personal taste.

Ingredients:
- 4 Tbsp Vegetable Oil (because of the higher smoke point)
- 4 Soup Cut Beef Shanks (at least 1" inch thick)
- Emeril's "Essence" seasoning; to lightly coat each shank
- 2 Lg. Onions, finely chopped
- 2 -3 Ribs Celery, finely chopped
- 2 – 3 lg. Carrots finely chopped
- ½ lb. Button Mushrooms, chopped
- 8 Cloves of Garlic, smashed, (or 2 TBSP minced garlic)
- 2 1/2 Cups of Dry Red Wine (I prefer Chateau St. Michelle Merlot. It makes a big difference in the final taste)
- 3 Tbsp. Tomato Paste
- 1 Can Crushed Tomatoes (15 oz.)
- 2 Cups Beef Stock
- ¼ cup Chopped Basil
- ¼ Cup Chopped Parsley
- 3 Bay Leaves
- 8 Sprigs of Thyme, chopped
- 2 Sprigs of Rosemary, chopped
- (Kosher or Sea) Salt and Pepper to taste

Procedure
1. Heat the vegetable oil in a large Dutch oven over high heat until very hot. While waiting on this, season both sides of the shanks evenly with Essence and transfer to the Dutch oven, Brown on both sides (Don't over crowd the pot). About 3 – 4 minutes per side. Transfer to a plate and set aside.
2. Add the onion, celery, carrots and mushrooms to the Dutch Oven and cook, stirring occasionally for even cooking and to get the pan juices mixed well with the vegetables. In about 7 minutes they should begin to caramelize.
3. Add the garlic, bay leaves, thyme and rosemary and cook for 2 minutes. (If you have fresh herbs, you can tie the herbs sprigs together with a bit of butcher twine instead of chopping) You will begin the smell the bouquet of herbs. Then slowly add the Red Wine and stir with a wooden spoon, scraping the bottom of the pot to help deglaze. The bits on the bottom of the pot are important to get into the liquid.
4. Add tomato paste, crushed tomatoes, beef stock, basil, parsley and salt and pepper. Stir in well. Return the shanks to the Dutch oven and bring to a boil. Lower heat to a simmer and cover. If you have upped the amount of beef, you may need to add a little extra liquid. Cook for about 4 - 5 hours, or until the shanks are tender, stirring occasionally and keeping the boys from pilfering spoonfuls. You will find that the meat has disappeared from the bones and now is in bite size pieces. Try to find and remove the Bay leaves. Serve with a salad of mixed greens and crusty artisan bread. You will want something to soak up the sauce in your bowl. Trust me.

Servings: 8. Preparation Time: 25 minutes. Cooking Time: varies; 4 hours.

Family Notes

Beefy Pockets

I love going to carnivals and fairs and eating food stuffed into a doughy mass of goodness. (A girl has got to have some sort of guilty pleasure.) This recipe reminds me of carnival foods. I have brought down the calories by not frying the pockets and by using fresh ingredients. It is a great way to get those hated vegetables into your kids. Next time you take the family to a carnival or fair, think of ways you can put a healthier spin on their favorite fun foods and make it at home. Change it up to suit your taste, but most of all have fun with your kids while you make them.

Ingredients:

- ½ Lb. Lean Ground Beef
- Package of Taco Seasoning, family favorite brand (you can make your own blend too)
- ½ Cup Frozen Vegetables, any you like, I prefer Mixed
- ¼ tsp. Minced Garlic
- 1/3 Cup Steak Sauce, your favorite
- 1 Cup Sharp Cheddar, yellow or white
- Store Bought Pizza Dough

Procedure

1. Preheat oven to 375 F degrees

2. In a sauté pan brown ups the beef, add in the taco seasoning, and vegetables and allow to cook until Vegetables begin to defrost.

3. Add in Garlic, steak sauce, mix to combine and cook another 5 minutes. Turn heat off and allow mixture to cool slightly.

4. Meanwhile roll out a piece of pizza dough about the size of your palm into a round shape. It does not have to be perfect, just big enough to put a spoonful of filling onto one-half of the dough.

5. Fill all your pizza rounds. Add Cheddar over the filling. Take the other half of the dough and fold over your filling, crimp the edges with a fork. Make sure the edges are well sealed and that you have not over stuffed your pockets.

6. Transfer to a Sil Pat (a commercially available silicone sheet) or parchment paper lined cookie sheet. Bake for 20-30 minutes or until the outer shell begins to turn a nice golden brown.

7. Pull out of the oven and allow to cool slightly. Serve.

Servings: Depending on size: 4 to 8 pockets. Preparation Time: 10 minutes. Cooking Time: 25 minutes.

Family Notes

BLT Rigatoni

All the goodness of a BLT sandwich in a dinner meal – how can that not be a family hit? The bacon (or Pancetta) makes a fine accompaniment to the pasta and chopped tomato sauce. The heat from the sauce and pasta will slightly wilt the Arugula. A little extra olive oil and cheese sprinkled on top makes this seem really decadent, but it is not. By no means is this a difficult meal to fix, which your kids can take a large role in preparing. I like the spicy bitterness of the Arugula in this dish. It makes it very complex on your palette. You can substitute Spinach if Arugula is not to your family's liking.

Ingredients:
- ¼ lb. Pancetta or Bacon
- 3 Tbsp. Extra Virgin Olive Oil
- 1 Sm. Onion, finely chopped
- 3 Garlic Cloves, finely chopped
- ½ Cup Dry White Wine
- 4 Ripe Tomatoes, cored and diced large
- Salt and Pepper, to taste
- ¾ lb of Rigatoni pasta
- ¼ Cup Chopped Fresh Basil
- 1 Bunch of Arugula, coarsely chopped
- ¾ Cup Parmesan Cheese

Procedure
1. In a skillet, or a 3qt. Sauté pan; cook the Pancetta using medium-high heat until crisp. Drain off excess fat on a paper towel. The Pancetta will have much less fat than bacon.

2. Cook Rigatoni in boiling, salted water until done according to box directions.

3. In a medium saucepan, heat 3 Tbsp of olive oil and add the garlic and onions. Cook until soft. This will take about 5 minutes. Then add the wine and bring to a simmer. After a minute add the tomatoes and season with salt and pepper to taste. Simmer over low, stirring occasionally, until thickened. This should take about 20 minutes.

4. Get your favorite family style large bowl and combine the cooked Rigatoni with the tomato sauce. Add the Pancetta and Arugula and toss well. Drizzle with a really good Olive Oil and sprinkle with the Parmesan.

Servings: 4. Preparation Time: 5 minutes. Cooking Time: 25 minutes.

Family Notes

Cheese Filled Meat Ball Sandwiches

Do you want a Meatball or a Patty? It's like arguing over pizza cut into sliced wedges or into squares. Meatballs are fun, but patties work really well on this sandwich and are easier for kids to eat. It's can be a way to get the kids involved and fun to have the family decide on meatballs or patties. I'm using ground turkey instead of ground beef to cut back on the fat content without hurting taste and protein. I'm blending the turkey with sausage. You will want bread that will stand up to this sandwich. We're filling these meatballs or patties with mozzarella cheese for an added treat. You could use Fontina cheese too. I am recommending marinara sauce as a time saver. You can use homemade spaghetti sauce, which goes to show, it's always a good idea to make a vat of the stuff and then freeze it in smaller containers.

Ingredients:
- 1 Lb. Ground Turkey
- 1 Lb. Sausage, either sweet or hot or a mix (cut out of casings)
- 2 Egg Yolks
- 1 Tbsp Chopped Fresh Parsley
- ¼ Tsp. Garlic Powder
- 1 Tsp Worcestershire Sauce
- 1 Tsp. Salt
- Fresh Ground Black Pepper (a few grinds will do)
- 1 Ball Fresh Mozzarella, cut into 6 equal pieces
- 2 Cups Shredded or Grated Mozzarella
- 1 Jar Marinara Sauce (32 oz.)
- 6 Sandwich Rolls, like Ciabatta or a hearty Multi- Grain

Procedure
1. Mix the turkey and sausage together in a bowl. Add in the next six ingredients and work gently together into a large ball. Then divide into 12 equal pieces. Flatten into a round patty and lay out six. Cover with a piece of the mozzarella then cover with the remaining six patties. You will have a little sandwich. Press the edges together to seal and sprinkle with salt and pepper.
2. If you want meatballs roll 12 balls and put a divot in the top of each with your thumb. Fill the divot with a piece of the mozzarella cheese. (You will need to cut the 6 pieces of cheese into 12.) Pinch over to keep the cheese from leaking out while cooking. Salt and pepper to taste.
3. In a heated, large sauté pan or skillet, add Olive Oil to coat. When it's hot, add as many of the patties (or meatballs) as you can -- without overcrowding the pan. Cook until lightly browned all over or both sides. They will finish cooking in the sauce.
4. While the patties are cooking, begin to heat your marinara sauce in a saucepan or deep skillet large enough to accommodate the patties. Add the cooked patties. Simmer on low heat long enough to blend the flavors and ensure the meat is completely cooked. At least 20 minutes.
5. Top the sauce with grated mozzarella and cook until cheese is melted, about 4 more minutes.
6. While you are waiting, slice and set out the rolls. You can toast them if you like. Put some sauce on the bread and then the patties. Top with more grated cheese and serve.

Servings: 4. Preparation Time: 20 minutes. Cooking Time: 20 minutes.

Family Notes

Couscous Salad with Grilled Shrimp Scampi

A great, quickly prepared dinner or hearty side salad. This is really a fantastic summer time treat too, especially since the cucumber provides a crisp and cool sensation in your mouth. The couscous, shrimp and cucumber make a hearty, yet light, combination. I've also made this dish with Quinoa to provide a little more nutrition. You can use some 'Old Bay' to season the shrimp if you want to change it up a little. The shrimp can be done on an outdoor grill or in a skillet. If you feel you need some greens and don't wish to prepare a side salad, serve on a platter with Romaine Lettuce, Watercress or Spinach and top with the Couscous and shrimp.

Ingredients:
- 2 Garlic Cloves, finely chopped
- 12 Shrimp, (at least medium sized, I prefer 31/40 count = large)
- ¼ Cup and 2 Tbsp. Extra Virgin Olive Oil
- 1 (10oz.) Box of Couscous
- 1 ½ Cups Chicken Broth (or Stock)
- 1 Lemon; Juice and grated zest
- ¼ Cup of Flat Leaf Parsley, chopped
- 1 Seedless Cucumber, peeled and chopped

Procedure
1. Toss half of the garlic in a medium bowl with 2 Tbsp of Olive Oil and the shrimp. Season with salt and pepper and quickly grill until cooked through. This will take about 2 minutes per side. Shrimp cooks really quickly -don't overdo it. Set aside when done.

2. Cook the Couscous in the chicken stock according to package directions, usually boiling for several minutes, letting stand and then fluffing with a fork. While this is being done, in a small bowl zest then juice the lemon. Toss in the rest of the garlic and parsley and diced cucumber and whisk in the remaining ¼ cup of olive oil. Put the couscous in a serving bowl and top with the dressing you just made. (Season to taste one last time). Top that with the shrimp and serve.

Servings: 4. Preparation Time: 5 minutes. Cooking Time: 25 minutes.

Family Notes

Inspired Moroccan Chicken

Many Moroccan dishes are prepared in clay tagine and slowly cooked over a long period of time. This can be a really fun cooking item to use in your kitchen. A tagine looks cool and brings a sense of exotic mystery and intrigue to your house. If you do not have one, my recipe only calls for a skillet and is a time saver. You will still get that taste of Morocco because of the spices. Your kids can go on adventurous trips without leaving your kitchen! Cooking should expose kids to different cultures. Encourage them to utilize this type of subject matter and information next time they have a book report or school project due.

Ingredients:
- Boneless Skinless Chicken Breast (1 per person and a extra one)
- ½ Cup Plain, non-fat Yogurt (Greek Style Yogurt works too)
- 1 Tsp Curry Powder
- 1 Tsp Cinnamon
- 1 Tbsp Mango Chutney
- 7 Tbsp Vegetable Oil
- 1 Tbsp. Honey
- Juice of ½ a Lemon
- Salt and Pepper to taste
- Golden Raisins (about a handful)
- Slivered Almonds (same handful or so)

Procedure
1. In a large bowl combine the yogurt, curry powder, cinnamon, mango chutney, vegetable oil, lemon juice and salt and pepper. Cut the chicken breasts into 1" chunks and place in the liquid mixture. Mix to coat well. It's better if you let it marinate in the fridge for at least 30 minutes.

2. Heat a non-stick skillet and cook the chicken pieces, being careful not to overcrowd the pan. You may need to cook in batches depending how big your skillet is and how much chicken you've used. During the cooking process add the raisins, almonds and honey.

Servings: 4. Preparation Time: 10 minutes. Cooking Time: 30 minutes.

Family Notes

Kid's Beefy Burritos

To get your kids interested, set up a taco bar with them. It's much more fun. Place the tortillas, ground beef, all your garnishes, cheese and the lettuce in separate bowls, along side dishes and utensils. Let everyone make his or her own burritos.

Kids love the taste of tacos, but not necessarily the taco shells. They break when bitten into and all the fillings drop out. The shell makes them hard to eat and a bigger clean up for parents. This is a basic taco recipe that we are wrapping in a soft corn tortilla. You get the same taco taste without the hassle! Plus corn provides certain health benefits and addresses dietary issues concerning wheat or flour. For instance, many corn tortillas are Gluten Free. I've made a version of this recipe in my family cooking classes and it is always a big hit. It is great for weeknights because of its straightforward ease and use of everyday ingredients.

Ingredients:
- 1 Lb. Lean Ground Beef (90% lean)
- ½ Cup Onion, finely chopped
- 1 Tsp. Canola Oil
- 2 Tsp. Ground Cumin
- 2 Tsp. Chili Powder
- ½ tsp. Garlic Powder
- ½ Tsp Kosher Salt
- ½ Cup Water
- 8 Corn Tortillas (or 100% Whole Wheat or Flour)
- Chopped Tomatoes, sliced Avocado, diced Red Peppers, Sour Cream
- 2 Cups Red Leaf Lettuce, shredded (Spinach works well too.)
- 2 Cups Mexican Cheese Blend, shredded (Cheddar and Jack blends)
- ¼ Tsp Cayenne Pepper (optional for extra heat)

Procedure
1. Preheat your oven to 350 F degrees to warm the tortillas. This can also be done in the microwave. Just slightly dampen the shells before nuking for a few seconds.
2. On the stovetop, heat a skillet with the canola oil over medium heat and add the chopped onions. We are using canola oil because of its high smoke point. When the onions are translucent add the ground beef and brown evenly, stirring to break up the beef. You don't need to over brown the beef here. Add your spices and the water. Stir well and bring to boil. Reduce the heat and simmer for 8 – 10 minutes.
3. While you are waiting, heat your tortillas. It will take 3 –5 minutes in the oven and about 10 -15 seconds per shell in the microwave. Remove the ground beef and the tortillas from heat and allow everyone to create their own taco.

Servings: 6. Preparation Time: 5 minutes. Cooking Time: 10 minutes.

Family Notes

March Madness Maple Glazed Pot Roast

It is now a dried, shrunken, tasteless and dull brown piece of meat. What happened? You put the roast in the pot when it was rich looking with nice marbling and a sanguine color. You seasoned it well with sea salt and cracked pepper and maybe some garlic. Now it looks awful and has no palatable appeal. Have you ever had this problem with pot roast? I have. I've found a few additional ingredients, and searing the meat in a Dutch oven, will prevent this from happening and provide your family with a succulent and tasty meal.

I use 'March Madness" in the recipe title because I'm adding Maple Syrup to flavor the roast. Here in New England the maple sap starts running in March. It's still cold in most of the USA and Pot Roast is a welcome comfort food in the waning months of winter. And this is a really great meal to serve your family while they are gathered around watching college basketball. Maple Glazed Pot Roast will become a family favorite and will teach kids many basic cooking techniques and preparation methods.

Ingredients:
- 2-3 lbs. Boneless Chuck Roast (go bigger if your family is large enough)
- 1 Cup Orange Juice
- ½ Cup real Maple Syrup
- 2 Tbsp Worcestershire Sauce
- 1 Orange, zested
- ¼ Tsp Kosher Salt
- ¼ Tsp Pepper (fresh ground is best)
- 4 Medium Carrots, cut into to 2" pieces
- 4 Celery ribs, cut into 2" pieces
- 1 Onion, roughly chopped
- 2 Large Potatoes, peeled and quartered
- 2-3 Parsnips cut in the pieces
- ½ lbs of Turnip, peeled and cut into chunks

Procedure
1. Put a thin layer of Olive Oil in the bottom of a heated cast iron Dutch Oven. Brown the roast evenly on all sides. While this is happening, combine the orange juice, maple syrup, Worcestershire sauce, orange zest and salt and pepper. When browned, pour over the roast and bring to a boil. Reduce heat to a simmer and put the lid on the pot. Let it go for an hour.
2. Add the carrots, celery, onion, parsnips and turnip and re-cover. Simmer for 20 minutes.
3. Then add the potatoes and cook for another 20 minutes or until the veggies are tender to a fork. The parsnips and turnip are optional depending on your family's taste. Add more potatoes if you're not using them. Remove roast and let rest for a few minutes before slicing. Serve with pan juices.

Servings: 6. Preparation Time: 20 minutes. Cooking Time: 40 minutes.

Family Notes

My Mom's Spaghetti Casserole

OK every family needs a weird casserole in their recipe box and this is my Mom's. You may turn your nose up to it at first, but DON'T pass this one up. I promise everyone you serve this too will beg for more, and it gets even better the next day.

Ingredients:
- 1 to 1 ½ lbs Ground Beef
- 15 oz. Canned Stewed Italian Tomatoes
- 1 Jar Plain Tomato Sauce
- 2 Cups Burgundy Table Wine (divided)
- 3 Tbs. Granulated Sugar
- 1 lb. Angel Hair Pasta
- 1 lb. Velveeta Cheese, grated
- 4 Tbs. Butter

Procedure
1. Pre-heat oven to 350 F degrees.
2. Butter a 2qt. casserole dish
3. In a 3 qt. Sauce pan or Sauté pan, brown the ground beef.
4. Add the stewed tomatoes, half of the tomato sauce, 1 cup of the wine, and 1 Tbsp of the sugar. Stir to combine, and simmer for about 45 minutes (every 15 minutes add a little more wine, and a Tbsp of sugar- continue until all the wine and sugar are incorporated)
5. Cook the pasta 2 minutes less than the package directs, drain and pour into the buttered 2 qt casserole dish, mix in the cheese and butter.
6. Reserve about a half cup of sauce, pour the rest into the pasta/cheese mixture, and stir in to combine. Top the casserole with the reserved sauce and place in the oven for 30 minutes. Serve.

Servings: 8. Preparation Time: 10 minutes. Cooking Time: 30 minutes.

Recipe Tips
Put the Velveeta in the freezer for 15 minutes before grating. It will help to actually grate it, otherwise you'll have a gooey mess on your hands. If you are pressed for time or all else fails, just cut the cheese up into small chunks and allow a couple more minutes to cook.

Notes: in this recipe it is crucial that you use Jug wine. A 'cheap' Burgundy table wine is best. And Velveeta; I know it sounds crazy but this recipe does not lend itself to upgrading to a fancy wine or any other cheese. I promise, use these 2 ingredients and you'll have a winner.

Family Notes

Eric's Pasta, Peppers and Italian Sausage

This is a go-to dish that we make regularly. It has never failed to please and heats up really well as a leftover casserole. Another one of our flexible dishes where you can add or substitute ingredients. Busy parents can be assured that basic components of this meal probably can be found in the pantry. When Eric makes this he never measures anything and it always comes out great. I say use a handful of cherry tomatoes; it really depends on how much you want. That's the beauty of this dish- it's versatility. Because your kids can judge for themselves what or how much of an ingredient they want to use. Sometimes Eric will even use up Spinach left over in the fridge. Just toss it in during the last few minutes of cooking. The Italian sausage can be either a sweet or hot or a mix of both. Eric really prefers red peppers to green. The red are much sweeter and it does not taste like that old sausage and peppers sitting a tin foil tub over a Sterno all day waiting for the banquet to start.

Ingredients:
- 1 lb Box of Pasta (Rotini)
- 1 lb. Italian sausage, usually 4 patties or 6 links (Sweet, Hot or a combo)
- 3 -4 Red Peppers, sliced
- ½ Pint (a handful) of Cherry Tomatoes
- 1 Onion, sliced into large pieces
- 1-Cup water
- 1 tsp Garlic sliced or minced (or a couple dashes of garlic powder)
- 2 Sprigs of Oregano, leaves removed from stems
- 2 Sprigs of Thyme, leaves removed from stems
- 4-6 Fresh Basil Leaves
- ½ Cup Ricotta Cheese
- Grated Parmesan Cheese on top (as much as you like)

Procedure
1. Bring 6 quarts of salted water to boil.
2. In a large sauté pan, chef pan or Dutch oven, (you'll need something with a lid) brown the sausage using a little oil. I break up the patties, or remove the sausage from the link's casing to brown and toss in the smaller pieces. Be careful not to over crowd the pan as you brown. The entire sausage link does not work well in this recipe. When the meat has slightly browned, drain off excess oil and return to heat. Drop in the onions and allow to cook until translucent. Toss in the cherry tomatoes, these will taste better if they are cooked till they get little bit of brown on the skins. When that happens, strip off the leaves of the Oregano and Thyme, add the Basil and a cup of water to the pot. If using dried herbs, a healthy sprinkle will do.) Stir and cover. Cook for about 20 minutes or until the peppers are soft and have cooked down.
3. The water for the pasta should be boiling by the time you have added in all your ingredients. Cook according to pasta directions.
4. When done, serve either family style or in individual bowls. Place the sausage and peppers over the pasta and top with a scoop of Ricotta cheese and a sprinkle of Parmesan cheese. Feel free to add crushed red pepper flakes to up the heat index!

Servings: 4. Preparation Time: 10 minutes. Cooking Time: 20 minutes.

Recipe Tips
I make a casserole with the leftovers. Here's where your creativity with ingredients or seasonings will come in handy. This way your family won't feel as if they are eating the same meal twice in the same week. Use a stone wear baking dish. I put a little bit of Extra Virgin Olive Oil on the pasta and then layer it in a baking dish and then top with the sausages and peppers (and your new seasonings). Then add a thin covering of Ricotta or Mozzarella cheese goes on the top. Sprinkle with more Parmesan. Cover with foil and bake at 350 degrees for about 30 – 40 minutes. The extra oil really adds to the nuance of flavor and keeps the pasta from becoming dried out, so use your best olive oil.

Family Notes

Pumpkin Risotto

I love Risotto because it is so versatile and you can add anything you like to it. I'm really puzzled why people seem to think it's so difficult or mysterious. **As long as you follow the method** the ingredients can change from season to season. Here is an easy recipe that anyone can do. It's great to do with kids because they can help you slowly add in the liquid and do some of the stirring. The whole process takes about 20 minutes, so be patient, relax, have fun and spread the workload. Kids love watching the rice turn from solid little masses into a rich creamy textured Risotto. The method is in the 1st 5 steps; the ingredients can change to your taste. Remember always use chicken or vegetable stock instead of water and keep your broth warm in a small saucepan as you begin to add it. Patience will yield you a much creamier result and allow the rice to fully cook. Have fun and get CREATIVE or better yet let your kids get creative.

Ingredients:
- 8 Cups Chicken (or Vegetable) Stock
- 2 Tbsp. Olive Oil
- 1/3 Cup Medium to finely chopped Yellow Onion (size depends on how pronounced you want the onion flavor to be)
- 1 Clove of Garlic, Finely Chopped
- 1 Cup Arborio Rice (do not substitute with regular rice)
- ½ Cup White Wine (optional)
- 1/2 Cup Cooked Butternut or Acorn Squash, mashed or diced
- 2 Tbsp of Parmesan Cheese (you can add as much or as little, but the better the quality -- the better the taste)
- 1/2 Tsp Chopped Fresh Rosemary or 1/4 Tsp dried
- 1/8 Tsp Ground Nutmeg
- 1/8 Tsp Kosher Salt

Procedure
1. Using a 3qt. Sauce Pan heat the stock over Medium-High heat
2. In a 3 qt. Sauté pan, heat Olive Oil, add the Onions and Garlic, sauté until translucent.
3. Add the rice and cook a few minutes allowing the rice to get coated and begin to turn translucent. Add the wine now, and allow to reduce until you can't see any liquid.
4. Add 1/2 Cup of the warmed chicken stock, stir continually until all the broth has been absorbed.
5. Continue to add the broth in 1/2 cup increments, stirring and allowing each addition of broth to be absorbed before the next increment of liquid goes in. **This is where your kid(s) come in handy.**
6. Once all broth has been absorbed, you should have a rich creamy mass of Risotto. Pull it off the heat and add in the remaining ingredients, stir to combine and serve.

Servings: 6. Preparation Time: 10 minutes. Cooking Time: 25 minutes.

Recipe Tip:
Wine is a perfectly acceptable addition since all the alcohol burns off and you are left with an intense flavor of the grape. Always use wine you would drink, never use "cooking wines".

Family Notes

Rose Marie's Family's Homemade Goulash

This recipe came from a friend whose family has loved it for a couple generations. It has been eagerly shared from parent to child and exemplifies our point of sharing memoires over meals. Rose Marie's grandparents are of Eastern European / Jewish descent. This is an Americanized version of their homemade style goulash. By definition this is not a "Goulash", it is more like an American style Sloppy Joe. Rose Marie tells us this was one of her favorites when she was a child and she lovingly calls this recipe "Slumgolian". It's comfort food nonetheless. We'd like to thank Rose Marie Bauer and her family for sharing this simple, warming and hearty meal!

Ingredients:
- 1 Lb. Ground Chuck
- 1 Small Onion Diced
- ½ cup Green Pepper (Red Pepper works too, and it's a little milder)
- ½ Bottle Ketchup
- 1 Can Tomato Paste
- 1 Cup Water
- 1 Tbsp Sugar
- ½ Lb. Macaroni (about half a box)

Procedure
1. In a large saucepan with a lid, cook the onion until it begins to sweat, then add the ground beef and begin to brown. Add the peppers.
2. When meat is browned and peppers begin to wilt, add the rest of your ingredients. Mix well.
3. Cook on the stove over medium – low heat, covered until the macaroni is tender. Add water as needed during this process.

Servings: 8. Preparation Time: 5 minutes. Cooking Time: 25 minutes.

Family Notes

Sausage & Pepper
Submarine Sandwiches

Where Eric grew up in New York these long sandwiches were called submarines. In Connecticut they call them 'Grinders" (even though Connecticut has a Sub base and New York State does not) Go figure. Use any name to get your kids to eat them. At least they taste good and you can make them at home and regulate the contents.

Ingredients:
- 3 Sweet Italian Sausage Links
- 3 Hot Italian Sausage links
- 2 Tbsp Olive Oil
- 2 Garlic Cloves, crushed
- 1 Large Onion, thinly sliced
- 2 Red Peppers, seeded and thinly sliced
- 1 Pepper – a variety as hot as you can stand
- Salt and Pepper (optional to taste)
- 2-3 Marinated Sweet Peppers, from a Jar (for the marinated flavor)
- 3 Tbsp Italian Dressing (or a oil and vinegar mix)

For the Bread:
- 4 Crusty Portuguese Rolls (or other 8 inch oblong roll)
- 1 Tbsp Olive Oil
- 3 Tbsp Butter
- ¼ Tbsp Garlic Powder
- ¼ Tbsp Each Chopped Fresh Herbs; Oregano, Parsley, Thyme

Procedure
1. Slice the sausages lengthwise and place in a sauté pan over medium-high heat. Add about 1 inch of water and bring to a boil. Cover and reduce heat, simmering for 10 minutes. Slicing the sausage makes it easier to eat and boiling removes a high percentage of the fat without the lot greasy splatter.
2. While the sausage is cooking, in a second skillet, over medium high heat, add oil and your garlic. In a minute or two when it becomes aromatic, add the onions, and peppers. Cook till soft. If you want, add salt and pepper here.
3. Drain the sausage and return to the pan. Bring up the heat to medium high and add a drizzle of oil. Brown and crisp the sausage. Combine the sausage with all the peppers and the dressing in a bowl and toss.
4. Split and butter the rolls and place under a broiler or in a toaster oven. When lightly golden, remove and sprinkle on the garlic powder and the chopped herbs. If you don't have fresh, an Italian Blend will work. Lay out your rolls and top with the sausage and peppers.

Servings: 6. Preparation Time: 10 minutes. Cooking Time: 20 minutes.

Family Notes

Eric's Sautéed Chicken and Black Olives over Orzo

Another *Go-To* favorite. Orzo is that tiny 'birds eye' pasta so good in soups, stews and in this dish. For some reason, orzo seems less filling than regular sized pasta shapes. It is important to get a good sear on the chicken. But be careful, you don't want to overcook them, and because they are cut in ribbons, or strips, they will cook really quickly. The time in the pot will cook them even more, so just get a good golden brown sear and begin to add the rest of the ingredients. If you are using real olives as opposed those in the can (and I would unless your kids have an aversion to the taste) you will notice the tangy pungency of the type of olive. Combined with the orzo and chicken it is really quite delicious.

Ingredients:
- 1.5 Lbs. Chicken Breast, sliced in strips (or use chicken tenders)
- 3 oz. Sliced Black Olives (pitted Kalamata works really well too)
- 8 oz. Orzo (about half a box)
- 12 oz. Can of Diced Tomatoes (nothing wrong with fresh if can get them)
- ¼ tsp each of Thyme, Oregano, Marjoram, Basil
- Clove Garlic (crushed)
- Salt & Pepper to taste
- Olive Oil
- Bunch of Kale or Chard (optional)

Procedure
1. Bring about 6 quarts of salted water to a rolling boil. The water for the pasta should be boiling by the time you have prepped all your ingredients. Cook according to pasta directions. Reserve about a coffee cup of water. Drain well.

2. While you are waiting for the pot to boil, heat a stainless sauté pan with a coating of olive oil poured in. Cut the chicken breast into ribbons (unless you bought chicken tenders hopefully when on sale). When the oil shimmers add the crushed garlic. As that becomes aromatic, add your chicken pieces careful not to overcrowd the pan. Flip to ensure even browning. After all the chicken has browned-- it won't be cooked through yet—add your diced tomatoes and olives. Be cautious as to how much juice from the tomato can you use. You don't want this to turn soupy. The juice from the olives is not an issue unless you're using canned, then drain the juice. Adjust your heat and simmer. Add in the herbs, adjusting to taste. Cook for about 15 to 20 minutes then add on top of your cooked and drained orzo. If the contents of the sauté pan start looking a little dry, add some water from the cooking orzo. The starch and salt given off from the pasta will be a better addition than plain water.

Servings: 4. Preparation Time: 10 minutes. Cooking Time: 30 minutes.

Family Notes

Tuna Puttanesca and Penne

Another very simple family pleaser and a great alternative to the usual' Italian dinner" because we've added Tuna. It's hard not to like tuna from a can even though it has become so mundane. This recipe spices it up. There are companies that can their tuna in Olive Oil. This type of oil packed tuna adds a little something extra in taste and consistency to the sauce. Make the effort to look for a Solid White or Yellow Fin Tuna packed in olive oil. It does make a difference. You can also use a grilled tuna steak. Add about a cup of red wine (Merlot, perhaps because of its character) and this can become a romantic meal for parents. This is a very quick meal using readily available ingredients that seems so much more complicated when you actually serve it.

Ingredients:
- 1 lb. Penne Pasta (any large pasta will do)
- 1 Tbsp. Extra Virgin Olive Oil
- 1 or 2(6oz.) Can(s) of Oil packed Tuna (lightly drained)
- 4 Garlic Cloves
- 3 Tbsp. Capers, drained and chopped
- Bunch of Kalamata Olives, pitted and chopped
- 1 (28oz.) Can Diced Italian Tomatoes
- Flat Leaf Parsley, coarsely chopped
- Red Pepper Flakes to taste (if desired)

Procedure
1. Bring a large pot of salted water to boil to the pasta. Salt really works wonders to improve the flavor of the pasta, so don't skip on this part. Cook pasta until al dente.

2. While this is happening, heat a deep skillet-- or sauté pan -- over medium heat and coat the bottom with olive oil.

3. Add the tuna, flaking it with a wooden spoon or fork as you put it in the pan. The better quality tuna you have the more you will want to use, which is why I say use 1 or 2 cans. A single tuna steak would also do.

4. Add the garlic and cook for 3 – 4 minutes. Stir in the capers and olives and heat until everything is warmed through, maybe another minute.

5. Stir in the tomatoes and the parsley and simmer—on low—for about another 5 minutes. By this time the pasta should be done, or close to it. So add about a ladle full of the pasta water to the tomato sauce. Drain the pasta well. Combine the pasta with the sauce and toss. Serve with your favorite grated cheese and/ or Crushed Red Pepper flakes.

Servings: 6. Preparation Time: 5 minutes. Cooking Time: 20 minutes.

Family Notes

Won't Hold You Up Turkey Chili

I've always wondered why the old Texas cowboys never used turkey for their chili. Maybe they did and Hollywood insisted on making us believe they only ate beef chili. I mean you never saw John Wayne, Jimmy Stewart, Randolph Scott, or any of the other great cowboy actors walking around eating a plate of beans with a bunch of wild turkeys off in the distance. I'm sure a turkey or two found its way into a cast iron pot with the peppers and beans considering the wild turkey's range is from the Texas panhandle up through Montana (and eastward up thru New England). So if any of your friends, or your kid's friends, say this isn't an authentic chili, you tell them that. Anyway, ground turkey is a fine alternative to ground beef in chili. The turkey is mild and becomes infused with the spices and other ingredients you've put in your chili pot. And turkey is high in protein and has a lower fat content than beef. Variety in a diet is an excellent way to stay healthy.

We have purposely included two ways to make chili: this one is very quick and easy, and perfect after a long work day. This quick turkey chili recipe won't hold you up and does not need to stew all day. It is also extremely kid friendly. It's loaded with protein and fiber and your kids definitely can help with the prep and selecting some of the ingredients. So get your cowpokes in the kitchen and 'Stick 'em up!'

Ingredients:
- 1 lb. Ground Turkey
- ½ Tsp Cumin
- 1 Tsp. Cinnamon
- Salt & Pepper, to taste
- 1 Can Kidney Beans, rinsed (15 Oz.)
- 1 Can Black Beans, rinsed (15 Oz.)
- 1 Jar of your favorite Salsa (15 Oz.)
- ½ to 1 Cup Water
- Wheat Tortilla Chips
- Shredded Cheese (your favorite)
- Reduced Fat Sour Cream

Procedure:
1. Preheat a 3-quart Sauté pan on medium. Combine the turkey, and the cumin, cinnamon, salt and pepper in a bowl. Add the Turkey mixture to the hot pan, breaking up as you go. Brown the meat evenly. Then add in your beans and salsa, stirring to combine. Lastly add in the water. You may need anywhere from a ½ cup to a full cup of water during the rest of the cooking process. Allow to cook on a low simmer for 30 minutes.

2. Ladle into bowls and serve with a decent portion of shredded cheese, followed by a dollop of sour cream. Serve alongside the Tortilla chips.

Servings: 8. Preparation Time: 15 minutes. Cooking Time: 30 minutes.

Family Notes

Slow Cooked Turkey Chili

This is our version of a traditional chili. This is a continual crowd pleaser because of its versatility and adaptability. These are usually basic ingredients to most chili. I have used ground turkey instead of ground beef because it's leaner and has fewer calories. It's never a bad idea to put variety in your family's diet either. There is virtually no taste difference between ground beef and turkey in a chili.

Ingredients:
- 2 Lbs. Ground Turkey (browned)
- 1 Medium Onion, diced
- 2 Green Bell Peppers, diced
- 2 Cups Chopped Celery
- 2 Cans of Diced Tomatoes (28 oz. Each can)
- 1 Can Whole Peeled Tomatoes (28 oz.)
- 1 Tsp Ground Cumin
- 1 Tsp Chili Powder
- 1 Can Pinto Beans, drained (14 oz. can)
- 1 Can Black Beans, drained (14 oz.)
- 1 Can Kidney Beans, drained (14 oz.)
- 1 packet chili seasoning mix or ¼ tsp each of the following, Cayenne, Garlic Powder (fresh chopped garlic cloves are better —Sauté them with the onions), Oregano, Thyme, Paprika, Salt.
- Shredded Cheddar Cheese and Sour Cream (as a topping)

Procedure
1. Heat a large pot over medium heat. While doing so, brown the ground turkey in a large Sauté Pan. Feel free to mix a pound of beef with a pound of ground turkey. (Pork and veal work well too.) There will be hardly any excess fat to worry about. If there seems to be too much fat in the pan, simply drain off excess.
2. In the heated pot, add the onions, chopped peppers and celery. Sauté briefly until the onions begin to weep. Stir in both cans of tomatoes.
3. Add the cumin and chili powder. Use as much as you like, depending on your tolerance to heat. Cook for about 8 minutes. Then add the beans, meat and the rest of your seasonings. Stir well. Partially cover and leave to simmer for 4 hours.

This recipe lends itself to a lot changes. You can use red peppers instead of green or a combination. You can use steak, diced in bite size pieces. A zucchini cooks nicely in the pot also. You can add Jalapenos. If you like a smoky taste, 1tsp (or 2) of Chipotle flakes. And I'm not kidding when I say toss a bar of dark chocolate in the pot. (First break into pieces if you do.). And the left overs taste better the next day.

Serve with the cheddar cheese and sour cream.

Servings: 8. Preparation Time: 20 minutes. Cooking Time: 2-3 hours.

Family Notes

Chapter 9
Salads

Elisabeth's Heirloom Tomato Herb Salad

Don't be fooled by the short list of ingredients and amount of preparation, this can be a gourmet quality salad. It's something littler kids can prepare too--no measuring required! Just use some of the freshest, best tomatoes you can get. Nothing compares to a summer ripened tomato. And really try to buy the organic heirloom tomatoes in different colors. Aside from their incredibly better taste, the color variations are much more striking and picturesque on the platter. This is a must for late summer dining!

Ingredients:
- 4 or 5 Heirloom Tomatoes (variety of colors and sizes)
- 1 Ball of Mozzarella (fresh is best)
- Fresh Herbs (to taste)
- Olive Oil
- Kosher Salt and (optional) fresh cracked Black Pepper (to taste)

Procedure
- Slice as many tomatoes as you think you will eat and arrange on a platter.
- Lay fresh Mozzarella slices between the tomatoes
- Sprinkle on top fresh herbs (to taste). We use Oregano, Basil, Tarragon and Thyme. Sometimes Elisabeth insists on Rosemary and it is actually quite good. If at all possible use fresh herbs, there is just so much more taste and visual appeal than in the dried herbs.
- Sprinkle Sea Salt over the Tomato slices (again to taste).
- Drizzle with Extra Virgin Olive Oil.
- Let sit for a while so that the flavors have a chance to meld together.

Servings: 6. Preparation Time: 5 minutes.

Family Notes

Lee and Elisabeth's Salad

Elisabeth actually came up with this recipe all by herself one day while at her grandmother's (who always encourages her grandchildren to try new kinds of fruits and vegetables). Romaine lettuce is darker than iceberg yet still has a mild taste that kids won't mind. Plus it's stiff enough for dipping which little kids seem to enjoy. I haven't specified amounts of the Lettuce, Olive Oil and Tomatoes since it really depends on appetite and/or how many people might partake in this salad. The other proportions remain the essentially the same.

Ingredients:
- Romaine Lettuce
- Cherry Tomatoes
- 1/8 Cup White Vinegar
- 2 Cups Cold Water
- Extra Virgin Olive Oil (First Cold Press)
- 1 Fresh Lemon (half for slices, half for juice and zest)

Procedure
1. In a bowl, wash the lettuce and tomatoes in a mixture of 2 cups of cold water and 1/8 cup of vinegar. Rinse with more cold water and dry. If you have a salad spinner, it makes quick work of the drying.

2. Elisabeth prefers that the 'dressing' be put on the side since she likes to dip the lettuce and tomatoes and squeeze drop of juice from the lemon slice. You can also drizzle it over the salad. Another method is to pour in a small bowl 2-3 teaspoons of Olive Oil, mix with juice from the lemon half and a bit of Salt and Pepper. Pour over the Romaine and tomatoes and top with the zest of half a lemon. The zest contains beneficial essential oils and is very fragrant which dresses this salad up.

Servings: 4. Preparation Time: 5 minutes.

Recipe Tip:
This offers an excellent way for toddlers to become accustomed to picking up and eating fresh vegetables.

Family Notes

Who's Waldorf Salad?

I love New York City. Even having spent many years living there I am still in awe of that place. It's the greatest city in the world. One of the things I really love is the history in that town. There is a strong sense of cultural development and it exemplifies how our nation grew up. The architectural look of the skyscrapers and how they evolved are evident even amongst hidden colonial gems like Fraunces Tavern or Trinity Church and the homier sections of town like The Village and Brooklyn. I am also amazed by some of the old hotels which still seem to keep the grand feeling of a time gone by.

Kids today have no idea what a Waldorf Salad is, or the cultural impact that 'salad' had during the 20th Century. It was invented in 1896 by the Waldorf+Astoria maitre d'hotel. Here's my take on an updated version of this famous chopped salad. The apples, walnuts, and creamy dressing are a nod to that venerable hotel in my favorite city: New York. I've used sour cream instead of mayonnaise (or plain Greek yogurt) as was used in the original recipe to coat the apples. The vegetable content, and thus the nutrient content, is really boosted in my version too. Hopefully your kids will ask why it's called a 'Who's Waldorf Salad' and you can tell them about a little bit of that old New York City High Society in days (now) gone by.

Ingredients:
- 6 Cups finely shredded Carrots
- 1 Cup Walnuts
- ¼ cup Golden Raisins
- ½ cup Granny Smith Apples, diced
- 1 Cup Reduced Fat Sour Cream
- 2 Tbsp. Apple Cider Vinegar
- 2 Tbsp. Honey (locally produced)

Procedure
1. In a large bowl combine the first four ingredients. In a smaller separate bowl combine the sour cream, vinegar and honey. Mix well, and then pour into the carrot mixture and toss to combine. Place in the refrigerator and allow it to marinate for at least 30 minutes. Overnight is better still. The marinating is necessary to improving the overall flavor and balance of this salad. This makes this a great buffet or party dish because you can make a day ahead of time.

Servings: 8. Preparation Time: 10 minutes. Inactive Time: 30 minutes.

Family Notes

Winter Citrus Salad (with Pomegranate)

This is a uniquely flavored fruit salad because of the syrup and a few key ingredients. Allspice and Star Anise seem to be rarely used and will be a pleasant surprise both in taste and presentation. (The star shapes of the pretty Anise spice and the Star Fruit provide a holiday feel.) Star Anise imparts a pungent licorice-like taste. I grated Fresh Ginger Root*, which has a spicy zing, unlike the dried or candied kind. The spiciness will become stronger as the salad sits. So be prepared if you are saving it for leftovers. You can buy whatever fruit is on sale. The Pomegranate is loaded with antioxidants, vitamins, potassium, folic acid and iron. It has become a super star in the field of nutrition. Usually you will see them in the markets from late fall to early winter. When you do, buy some and add the seeds to this citrus salad. (To avoid getting stained, cut off the ends and section the fruit into quarters, placing each in a bowl of cold water. With your fingers under the water, roll out the beautiful ruby-red, jewel-like juice sacks [called Arils]. Discard the pith and the skin. Strain the water and use the entire Arils). If you can't get Pomegranates, this recipe still works really well. It is a real treat during winter and a great way to get those fruit borne vitamins into your system.

Ingredients for Salad:
- 3-4 Oranges, Supremed*
- 1 Ruby Red Grapefruit, Supremed*
- 1 Star Fruit, sliced
- 3 Kiwi Fruit, peeled and sliced
- 1-2 (depending on how much salad you will want) Pear or Apple, sliced thin
- 1 Pomegranate if available (Arils only)

You will need to 'Supreme' the larger citrus fruit. This is not as difficult as it sounds. A Supremed fruit is the segment of a citrus fruit without the skin and the white pith membrane that surround the fruit. This is a good technique to learn and a cool word to have in your arsenal of cooking terms. Our Citrus fruit section tells you how.

To Make the Syrup:
- 2 Oranges, Juiced and Zested
- 2 Limes juiced and Zested
- 1-Cup Sugar
- 4 Whole Star Anise
- 2 Tbsp. Fresh Grated Ginger*
- 1/8 Tsp. Allspice
- ½ Cup Water

Procedure:
Use a small saucepan or saucier and combine all the syrup ingredients, stirring occasionally. Cook until the sugar has dissolved. Remove from heat and allow to cool. Pour the cooled syrup over the fruit and allow time for the flavors to meld together, in the refrigerator, for at least two hours. Overnight is better.

Recipe Tip:
* **Fresh Ginger Root** can be frozen and used when needed, making it more economical. Just grate off whatever you need and stick in a freezer bag and back in your freezer. The best way to peel fresh ginger is by using a spoon to scrap off the outer skin. A knife removes too much of the actual ginger and it's expensive so you'll want to maximize it's yield.

Servings: 6. Preparation Time: 20 minutes.

Family Notes

Avocado-Mango Salad

This salad can be packed for a healthy quick lunch, toss in some tortilla chips and it makes as a great salsa.

Ingredients:
- ½ a Vidalia Onion, chopped finely, (optional)
- 1 Can of Beans, 15 oz. your choice (black, kidney, cannellini, etc.)
- 2 Vine Ripe Tomatoes, diced
- 1 Green Pepper, diced
- 1 15oz can corn, water drained from it
- Fresh Parsley, chopped fine (to taste)
- 2 Avocados, peeled and diced
- 1 Mango, diced or 1 pomegranate seeded, or even 1 granny smith apple peeled, cored, and diced. (Feel free to experiment; you could add berries, or papaya. Always buy what is in season, as it will cost you less.)

Dressing:
- ¼ cup Extra Virgin Olive Oil
- 2 tablespoons Lime Juice
- 1 Teaspoon Sugar
- 1 Garlic Clove, minced

Procedure:
1. Combine all the salad ingredients, mix gently to combine.
2. Whisk the dressing ingredients together, until the sugar has dissolved.
3. Toss dressing over salad, and gently combine.

Recipe Tip
You may serve the salad immediately, however, it is truly at its best when allowed to refrigerate for at least an hour and preferably over night, allowing the ingredients to become one and develop their flavors.

Family Notes

Tuna Salad Surprise

Growing up I thought the way my mother made Tuna salad was the only way it was done. Then to my surprise, I realized the way my mom made Tuna was NOT how Tuna salad was traditionally made. Traditional Tuna Salad uses no tomatoes or celery, but always seems to have onions. My mom never used onions, and I find raw onions will over power the tuna and take away from the taste. I love this Tuna Salad; it is so simple and so good. Four basic ingredients make up the entire recipe.

Ingredients:
- Can Tuna, packed in Water
- 1 Tomato diced
- 1 Stalk Celery, chopped finely
- ½ Cup Real Mayonnaise

Procedure
Combine all ingredients and let chill in the refrigerator for a minimum of 30 minutes. When chilled, assemble onto wheat toast, or serve with a side of Apple Sauce

Servings: 4. Preparation Time: 5 minutes. Inactive Time: 30 minutes.

Recipe Tips
I like my tuna cold, so I always keep my tuna cans in the refrigerator, that way when I want to make this salad the tuna is already cold and I can enjoy it quicker.

Family Notes

My Mom's Ham Salad

Don't cringe. Not every ham salad is horrible! Ham salad is one of those concoctions that has suffered from its popularity. You've seen it in a can, languishing at the deli, or sitting untouched at a picnic. Over the years it has been augmented to its' detriment with every conceivable ingredient you can think of. Still it is very popular, not difficult to make well, and a good way to use up left over ham.

My mom made ham salad this way all my life, especially during the summer. This old family recipe uses no onion. The real secret is the type of pickle and the type of mustard. Sweet Baby Gherkins impart such a different taste: sweet yet tangy and vinegary. They provide a crunch too. Pair this with a brown or a Dijon variety of mustard— not yellow. I love yellow mustards, just not in this recipe.

Ingredients:
- 4 Thick Ham Slices, diced and cubed into ¼ inch pieces
- 6 Hard-Boiled Eggs, crushed with a fork
- 3 Celery Stalks, diced
- ½ Cup Real Mayonnaise
- 1 Tbsp. Mustard (I like Grey's)
- 1 Tbsp Fresh Lemon Juice
- 1 Small Jar Sweet Baby Gherkin Pickles (about 16 oz), diced.
- Salt and Pepper to Taste

Procedure
1. Dice the ham, pickles and celery and drop in a serving bowl.
2. Fork mash the eggs and add them to the bowl.
3. Add the rest of the ingredients and combine well. Refrigerate for at least one hour—but overnight is better—before serving.

Servings: 6. Preparation Time: 10 minutes.

Family Notes

Chapter 10
Side Dishes

Cider & Cinnamon Braised Parsnips

This recipe was inspired by a recent trip to the Fore Street Restaurant in Portland, Maine. They serve these excellent parsnips as a side. The sweet tanginess of the apple cider went extremely well with the unique taste of the parsnip. They use the little tender ones and serve them while still sizzling in the pan. Of course, at Fore Street everything is cooked in a large brick oven, (which you can see from your table) so hot the flames look like orange liquid as they caress the burning oak logs.

Ingredients
- 1 lbs. Parsnip, cleaned, cut into equal sized pieces
- ¼ Tsp Cinnamon
- 1/4 Cup Apple Cider
- 1 Tbsp Butter

Procedure
1. Pre-heat oven to 450 F degrees.

2. Peel and chop the parsnips so that they will be all the about same thickness and length. Parsnips are funny since they can be really thick at the top and narrow down to a string. Do this simply to ensure even cooking.

3. Heat a sauté pan and add a pat of butter, coat evenly, then add your parsnips. Add the cider. Sprinkle evenly with cinnamon and cover, allowing the parsnips to braise for about 10 – 15 minutes, until they begin to get tender.

4. Then transfer the pan to your oven to roast the parsnips for about 10 minutes. (You may need to add a little extra cider.) Remove from oven when tender and they have begun to caramelize at the edges. There still should be some juice in the bottom of the pan.

Servings: 4. Preparation Time: 5 minutes. Cooking Time: 20 minutes.

Recipe Tips
I like to use a cast iron skillet to cook this in. I borrow a metal lid from one of my sauté pans to help in the braising process. I find that finishing the parsnips in cast iron is better because it holds the heat. (It will work on stainless, if you don't have a cast iron skillet.)

Another technique is to cook the parsnips on the grill. You prepare everything the same way, placing the parsnips evenly in the cast iron skillet and allow the closed grill to assist in the braising. Get your grill really hot. Cast iron works great on a gas or wood fired grill.

During the fall, or if you need to stretch this recipe for more diners, sauté a sliced apple with the parsnips.

Family Notes

Fall Casserole

A family favorite of mine and well suited for the entire autumn and winter seasons. This nourishing meal not only evokes memories of holidays, but of cold autumn days, football and active kids running around and kicking the leaf piles. It is a sweet dish, not cloying, full of fruits and root vegetables, but very much desert-like. And you won't need to put marshmallows on top of the sweet potatoes to get kids to eat this.

Ingredients:
- 5 Cups (1/4inch) Diced Sweet Potatoes (approx 2)
- 5 Cups Chopped Granny Smith Apples (approx 3)
- 1 Cup Sweetened, Dried Cranberries
- 1 ½ Cups Firmly Packed Brown Sugar
- 2 Tsp Cinnamon
- ¼ Tsp. Sea Salt
- ¼ cup Butter, cut into tsp sized pats
- 1-Cup Quick Cooking Oatmeal
- ¼ cup Flour
- ½ cup Melted Butter

Procedure
1. Preheat oven to 400 F degrees.
2. For the Casserole: Combine the Sweet Potatoes, Apples and Dried Cranberries in a bowl big enough to accommodate them and allow room for mixing. In a separate, smaller bowl, combine a ½ cup of the Brown Sugar, 1 tsp Cinnamon and Salt. Add this to the Sweet Potato/Apple bowl and toss well. Then spoon the mixture into a 13"x9"x2" baking dish and dot with the butter pats.
3. For the Topping: using another small bowl, pour in the Oatmeal, 1 cup Brown Sugar, the Flour, and 1tsp. Cinnamon and then combine. Then stir in the melted butter and spoon evenly over the top of the Sweet Potatoes and Apples.
4. Bake covered for 45 minutes and then another 30 minutes –uncovered-- to give you the crispy topping.

Servings: 8. Preparation Time: 15 minutes. Cooking Time: 45 minutes.

Recipe Tip:
I've actually eaten left overs of this for breakfast. Just re-heat in the oven safe dish you made it in.

Family Notes

Minted Stuffed Tomatoes

When tomatoes are at their peak and over-abundant this recipe will give you something to sing about. It's always great to come up with different ways to utilize a bumper crop of produce. You can utilize not so great winter tomatoes in this recipe, because you're baking them, there by intensifying their wonderful flavor. They will turn out just as well. Living on the East Coast, any time I can inject some summer feel into my winter meals I am a happy camper. Lastly it pays to use the best olive oil you can get your hands on.

Ingredients:
- 4 Large Fresh Tomatoes
- 1 Cup Fresh Whole Wheat Bread Crumbs
- ½ Cup Fresh Mint, finely chopped
- ¼ Cup Packed Light Brown Sugar
- 2 Tbs. Unsalted Butter, melted
- Extra Virgin Olive Oil (Best quality)

Procedure
1. Preheat the oven to 400 F degrees
2. Core each tomato with a small paring knife, but do not go all the way through to the bottom.
3. In a bowl combine bread crumbs, mint, sugar, butter, salt and pepper.
4. Fill the cavities of each tomato, drizzle the tops with a little olive oil and bake for 10-15 minutes.

Servings: 4. Preparation Time: 5 minutes. Cooking Time: 30 minutes.

Family Notes

Eric's Oven-Roasted Home Fries

You may never buy frozen French Fries again. These potatoes are cut like steak fries so they will absorb much less oil because of the larger pieces. There is no let down in flavor, either. Sometimes I will add Bell Peppers with the Onions for more taste. Cut them big so that they do not cook away to nothing. Roasting sweet potatoes alongside the potatoes brings out the carmalization and the sweet potatoes become oozy and tasty turning bright orange and an intense brown. Sweet potatoes are one of the healthiest vegetables you can eat and incredibly flavorful and useful especially when roasted in this manner. You can leave out the bell peppers and sweet potatoes if your kids balk at these vegetables, but making this dish is a good way to get them to try a small piece.

Ingredients:
- 2 lbs. New Red Potatoes, cut into strips (Baking Potatoes may be used)
- 1 or 2 Sweet Potatoes, cut lengthwise into strips
- 1 Clove Garlic, sliced or minced (or use garlic powder if you're in a pinch)
- 1 lg. Onion, chopped large
- 1 Red or Green Bell pepper, sliced into strips (optional)
- ¾ Tsp. Rosemary (dried or fresh)
- 2 Tbsp, Olive Oil
- Sea Salt and Pepper to taste

Procedure
1. Pre-heat oven to 400 F degrees.
2. Peel your potatoes and sweet potatoes. Using a large, rimmed baking sheet or roasting pan, combine potatoes, peppers, onions and sweet potatoes with Olive Oil and seasonings. Mix or toss to coat evenly. Bake till tender, about 1 hour.

Servings: 4. Preparation Time: 10 minutes. Cooking Time: 1 hour.

Family Notes

Tomato & Blue Cheese Tart

Blue cheese is pungent and aromatic and pairs well with so many things. The blue is actually a mold spore. Some of the best blue cheeses are still aged in caves as they were centuries ago. Making this Tart in the late summer is a treat when the tomatoes are especially tasty. Cook it on a cool September night when you can't figure out how to use all the extra tomatoes you have. You can get vine-ripened tomatoes year round (at your local mega markets) so this not a seasonal dish. Even though the mega market tomatoes can be bland, the blue cheese and a high quality Olive Oil and Sea Salt will save the day.

Ingredients:
- 1 Pie crust, 9 Inch
- 1 Tbsp Extra Virgin Olive Oil
- Sea Salt & Fresh Ground Pepper
- 8 oz. Whole Milk Ricotta Cheese
- 4 oz. Blue Cheese, crumbled
- 1 Large Egg
- 3 Medium Vine –Ripened Tomatoes, thinly sliced
- 7 oz of Mixed Salad Greens (bitter greens work well with the tart)
- 1 Lemon, zested and juiced

Procedure
1. Pre-heat oven to 400 F. Unroll the piecrust and press into a 9inch tart pan. Use a fork to prick the piecrust evenly across the entire surface. Then brush on about 1 Tbsp of olive oil and sprinkle with sea salt and pepper. Bake for 10 minutes.

2. While the crust is baking, stir together in a medium bowl the Ricotta, Blue Cheese and egg until combined. Remove the tart from the oven and immediately prick with a fork in a few places. This will remove any air bubbles. Then spoon the cheese mixture into the tart shell and top with the sliced tomatoes. Season with salt and pepper to taste and bake for 25 minutes. Let cool before serving.

3. Add a side salad, toss the washed salad greens in a large serving bowl with Olive Oil. Then toss in the lemon juice and the zest and sprinkle with salt and serve.

4. A complete meal with the cheese protein and vegetables and a little bit of carbohydrates from the piecrust.

Servings: 8. Preparation Time: 10 minutes. Cooking Time: 35 minutes.

Family Notes

Tomatoes with Blue Cheese Buttermilk

Ever need to find something to do with left over Buttermilk? I always find I need a ½ cup for some baking recipe and then I have the remainder of the quart sitting in the fridge. Aside from buttermilk pancakes I can't figure out what to with it before the expiration date. This recipe lends itself to year round usage. In the late summer you can use heirloom or vine ripened tomatoes. Make it in winter with cherry tomatoes. Either way it gives your family a great side dish. It is easy for your kids to make as well. I will set it out as a hors d' oeuvres when have bunch of them sitting around.

Ingredients:
- 1 Cup Crumbled Blue Cheese
- 3/4-Cup Buttermilk
- 2 Tbsp Extra Virgin Olive Oil
- 2 Tbsp lemon juice, plus the zest of the same lemon
- Kosher Salt and Fresh Ground Pepper (to taste)
- Pinch of Celery Seed
- 1 Bunch of Chives, Minced (optional. Add if you like the flavor. I find it helps this.)
- 2 Pints of red and yellow Cherry Tomatoes (I pint each) or 2 –3 Vine Ripened or Heirloom Tomatoes depending on size
- 1 Small Red Onion or 1 Shallot or ¼ cup of Leeks, minced

Procedure
1. Depending on your taste, you might find the red onion very strong and with some people it causes indigestion. Your teenagers won't want it on their breath. I like using a shallot or if you have them (the very underrated) leek. A leek has a flavorful, yet mild, onion taste and can be used in too many dishes to name. You will need to cook the Leek before using them in this dish. They are quick to sauté. If you're using the Blue Cheese Buttermilk tomatoes as a side dish you can cook a bunch of leeks. Use them as you would an onion in the main course.
2. To prepare the dressing, pour the blue cheese, buttermilk and olive oil in a medium bowl and stir together with a fork. Be careful here, you don't want to turn this in to a soup. The actual amount of buttermilk will vary depending on how many tomatoes you are using. You will need to mash up the blue cheese to get it fully incorporated. Then season with lemon juice, zest, celery seed, salt, pepper and the optional spices you decided upon.
3. Wash the tomatoes and pat dry. Slice into bite sized pieces. If you are using cherry or grape tomatoes, cut them in half lengthwise. Lightly season with a pinch of Sea Salt and pepper and place in a serving bowl. Pour enough of the mixture to lightly coat the tomatoes and toss. Serve with pitas cut into diamond shaped quarters or as a dinner side dish and garnish with some fresh parsley.

Servings: 4. Preparation Time: 10 minutes.

Family Notes

Vegetable Gratin

Think of this as sort of like scalloped potatoes but with less calories and fat and more nutrients. It is assembled like scalloped potatoes too, and if you have a mandolin it will make very quick work of thinly slicing the fennel and squash and potatoes. What makes it stand out are the Yukon Gold potatoes. They add more creamy goodness than if you used cream alone and the Yukon Gold potatoes mix well with the unique flavor and texture of the fennel. This is a fantastic way to introduce that wonderfully healthy, yet underutilized vegetable —Fennel — to your family.

Ingredients:
- ¼ Cup All Purpose Flour (unbleached)
- ¼ Cup Packed Light Brown Sugar
- 1 Tsp. Salt
- ½ Tsp. Black Pepper
- 1 Small Winter Squash (approx. 1 lbs. Use butternut, buttercup or acorn) peeled and sliced thin.
- 1 Yellow Onion, sliced thin
- 1 –2 Yukon Gold Potatoes (depends on size) peeled and sliced thin.
- 1 Small Fennel Bulb, sliced thin.
- 2-3 cups Milk or Cream (I use 2% milk and then dot the top of the gratin with unsalted butter pats before baking)
- ½ Cup Grated Parmesan Cheese (of course a little extra never hurts)

Procedure
1. Preheat oven to 350 F degrees.
2. Oil a 2 qt. or larger casserole dish. Using a small bowl combine the first 4 ingredients and set aside. Lay the first layer of squash, Onion, fennel and potato in the casserole dish. Then sprinkle 1/3 of the flour and spice mixture over top. Do the same with another layer of the vegetables and cover with another 1/3 of the flour and spice. Repeat till you have used all the ingredients. (The dish should be filled about 2/3 high—this will allow it not to bubble over in the oven). Press down the ingredients firmly in the dish. Now pour your milk into the casserole dish just until it comes half way up the sides of the casserole dish. For the topping liberally cover with the Parmesan cheese (and some butter if you choose).
3. Bake for 1.5 hours. Let stand for 15 minutes before serving. This dish works well reheated for leftovers, but Does Not freeze well.

Servings: 8. Preparation Time: 20 minutes. Cooking Time: 1 hour and 30 mins.

Family Notes

Cheddar-Cheese and Herbed Biscuits

This is my way of taking a biscuit and making it a little more nutritious than your average biscuit. The Fresh Herbs are wonderful in these biscuits. I love using Fresh herbs whenever possible, especially in the winter when I am missing the spring and summer harvest, they are a little pricy, but they are well worth it. It's easy to have your own herb garden, our herb chapter tells you how.

Ingredients:
- 2 Cups Whole Wheat Flour
- 1 Cup All Purpose Flour (unbleached)
- 1 Tsp. Baking Powder
- 1 Tsp. Baking Soda
- ½ Tsp Salt
- ½ Tsp Sugar
- ½ cup cold, Unsalted Butter, cut into small pats
- 2 cups Grated Cheddar Cheese, or any family favorite
- 2 Tbsp Fresh Sage (chopped)
- 2 Tbsp Fresh Thyme (chopped)
- ½ Cup Buttermilk
- ½ Cup 2% Milk (additional ½ cup may be needed depending on dough consistency)

Procedure
1. Preheat Oven to 375 F degrees
2. In a bowl whisk together the flours, baking powder and soda, salt, and sugar.
3. Using a pastry blender or a fork cut butter into the flour mixture until it begins to resemble coarse crumbs, you can also use a food processor, but be careful NOT to OVER MIX, you do not want to heat up the butter, and by over processing the butter into the flour you'll end up doing just that and coming out with a tough crust. Stir in Cheese and Herbs, then pour in Buttermilk and regular milk, stir with a fork until mixture just comes together to form a sticky dough.
4. On a lightly floured work surface pat the dough into a 1" thick round. Use a biscuit cutter, a round cookie cutter, or even an empty can, dipped in flour to cut out your biscuits. Transfer to a baking sheet.
5. In a small bowl stir together the egg and cream, wash the tops of each biscuit and bake 20-30 minutes.

Servings: 12. Preparation Time: 10 minutes. Cooking Time: 25 minutes.

Family Notes

Chapter 11
Soups

Left-Over Turkey Soup

Well, you've got a Thanksgiving turkey carcass with hunks of meat still on it and you don't know what to do. You don't really want to toss it in the garbage because that would be like throwing away money. Your kids won't go near it (unless you have boys who like disgusting things) because it looks awful – all cut and chewed-up looking with bones sticking out and replete with various colors ranging from light pink to a wide array of caramels and browns to almost white. Here's what you do. It's simple, inexpensive and we're loading it with vegetables so you don't need to force your family to eat a salad. This is a light soup but you could almost make it chowder. If you want it thicker, add a ¾ cup of lentils or Cannellini Beans. This boosts the heartiness and the protein content.

Eric does this all the time when he makes soups or stews. He puts in all kinds of root vegetables (and some leafy green ones too just for kicks) and lets the favors meld into an interesting, hearty and soul warming meal. You can make this all winter and feel free to substitute ingredients or quantities. If you don't have a whole turkey, a breast will work or substitute a Rotisserie Chicken from the market. It is a great way to expand your meals and your budget.

Ingredients:
- Turkey left overs with the bones. Boiled down to 7 cups of stock (about 1 hour).
- 3 Slices Bacon
- 1 Large Yellow Onion (diced)
- 2 Stalks of Celery
- 2 Red Potatoes (large) or 3 –4 small ones, peeled and quartered
- 1 Butternut Squash, peeled and diced
- 1 Zucchini (medium sized), chopped
- 2 Cups Chopped Swiss Chard (cutting out the stalks and ribs)
- 2 Cups of the turkey meat, diced to a bite size.
- 1 Tablespoon minced Fresh Sage
- 1 Tablespoon Fresh Thyme
- Salt and Ground Pepper (to taste- since you've used a turkey carcass you've already prepared for dinner, you will need to judge how much salt and pepper to add by your taste.)

Procedure
1. Strain Turkey stock into another pot. Let cool to touch before removing meat from the bones and set aside.
2. In a heavy bottomed stockpot, cook bacon over medium heat until browned. Stir frequently. When done set aside. Reserve only 1 tablespoon of the bacon fat in the stockpot, add diced onion and celery and sauté until soft. Do not brown.
3. Add the squash and turkey stock and meat and bring to a boil. Then simmer until tender, about 15 to 20 minutes. Then add the potatoes and zucchini. Partially cover the pot and stir occasionally until potatoes are soft.
4. Rough chop the fresh herbs and crumble the bacon into the soup. Add the chard. Simmer for another 5 minutes. Add Salt and Pepper and serve. As with all soup, its' even better the next day.

Servings: 10. Preparation Time: 1 hour. Cooking Time: 1 hour and 30 mins.

Family Notes

Roasted Winter Vegetable "Chowder"

If think Chowders are heavy and creamy and just made with corn or clams, then you must try my version of chowder. And while I say the bacon is optional in this recipe, I find it makes the soup extremely tasty, adding a whole new layer of flavors to the vegetables. Aside from the bacon, this is a vegetarian recipe. You can also substitute chicken stock instead of vegetable stock if you are not concerned about making this vegetarian recipe.

Ingredients

- ¼ lb Bacon, diced (optional)
- 1 Medium Yellow Onion, diced
- 4 Ribs of Celery, diced
- 2-4 Red Potatoes, peeled and diced
- 2-3 Carrots, peeled and cut into bite size pieces
- 1 1lb Butternut Squash, peeled, halved lengthwise, seeded, and cut into bite size chunks
- 7 Cups Vegetable Stock
- 2-3 Medium Zucchini, cut into bite size pieces
- 1 Bunch of Swiss Chard or Spinach, rough chopped
- Fresh Sage, minced, to taste
- Fresh Rosemary, rough chopped, to taste
- Fresh Thyme, to taste
- Salt and Pepper to taste

Procedure

1. In a heavy bottomed 6qt stockpot, cook the bacon (if using) over medium heat, stirring frequently, until browned. Remove with a slotted spoon to a plate. Set aside. Pour off all but 2 Tbsp of the bacon fat, and return the pot to medium heat.

2. (If not using Bacon) Add a Tbsp of Vegetable Oil to the pot, and allow to heat up, then add the onions, and celery. Sauté until the vegetables are soft, but not browned, about 3-5 minutes.

3. Toss in the Potatoes, Squash, Carrots, and vegetable stock and then bring to a boil. Reduce the heat to a simmer. Cover the pot and cook until the vegetables are fork tender, about 20 minutes.

4. Add the zucchini, Swiss chard, sage, rosemary, thyme, and reserved Bacon (if using). Cook for another 5-10 minutes

5. Add Salt and Pepper to taste, ladle into bowls and serve.

Servings: 10. Preparation Time: 15 minutes. Cooking Time: 35 minutes.

Family Notes

Cardamom-Parsnip Soup

Ingredients:

- 2 lbs. Parsnips, cut in half and then in half again
- A handful of Baby Carrots
- 4 tablespoons Extra Virgin Olive Oil (to roast vegetables with)
- Kosher Salt
- Fresh Black Pepper
- ½ Yellow Onion, finely diced
- 2 Celery Stalks, finely diced
- 1 tablespoon Extra Virgin Olive Oil (to sauté onions and celery with)
- 1 teaspoon Cardamom, divided
- 32oz. Vegetable Stock (usually 1 Box equals 32 oz.)
- 1½ - 2 Cups Milk or Cream
- Water (enough to thin out soup)

Procedure:

1. Preheat oven to 375 F degrees

2. Place parsnips and baby carrots on to a sheet pan, drizzle oil over the vegetables, generously sprinkle with salt and pepper. Coat the parsnips and carrots with the oil, salt, and pepper.

3. Roast for 30 to 45 minutes

4. Allow the vegetables to cool

5. In a 3qt saucepan, on medium heat, sauté the onions and celery, with a tablespoon of olive oil, until tender and translucent about 4 to 5 minutes, add salt and pepper to taste and ½ teaspoon of cardamom, mix to combine.

6. Add in parsnips and carrots, mix to combine.

7. Add in vegetable stock, bring to a boil, and then remove from heat. Using an immersion blender, blend until desired consistency has been reached. Add liquid if necessary.

8. Add in the milk and the other ½ teaspoon of cardamom. Mix to combine and adjust seasoning as needed.

Servings: 4 - 6. Preparation Time: 15 minutes. Cooking Time: 45 minutes.

Family Notes

Rosemary White Bean Soup

When the weather is turning colder soup is a must have dish. I can think of only a few better meals to make when the windows are iced over and the snow is coming down outside. Soup makes your home warm and aromatic. This meal is high in protein and fiber and low in fat. Check out how short the list of ingredients is! This is great soup to make for the family on a weekend or a snow day. Have it ready when your kids come inside from sledding and are freezing. It also serves as a nice soup for an adult dinner party with your friends because it is so very easy to make. You don't have to stress out over the first course. If you use canned beans you don't need to wait several hours to soak the beans. Just add up how many cans you need to open to a make pound.

Ingredients

- 1 lb. Dried White Cannellini Beans
- 4 Cups sliced yellow onions
- ¼ Cup olive oil (enough to cover bottom of pan)
- 2 Minced Garlic Cloves
- 1 lg. Branch of Rosemary
- 2 qts. Chicken Stock
- 1 Bay Leaf
- 2 tsp. Kosher Salt
- ½ tsp Ground Black Pepper

Procedure

1. In a medium bowl cover the beans with about an inch of water. Place in the refrigerator for at least 6 hours or overnight (or while at work).
2. When ready to begin cooking, drain the beans. Sauté the onions in the olive oil over low to medium heat using a large, heavy bottom stockpot. Cook until the onions become translucent, about 10 minutes. Add garlic and cook over low heat for another three minutes, being careful not to burn the garlic. Add the drained white beans, rosemary sprig, chicken stock and bay leaf. Cover and bring to a boil. Reduce heat and simmer for 30- 40 minutes or until the beans are very soft. Remove the rosemary sprig and bay leaf.
3. The soup is ready now (with a little salt and pepper). If you want to serve it a little fancier, or if our kids won't eat soup with whole beans in it, there are three easy methods to puree the soup. You can run the soup through a food mill, using the coarsest blade available. If you have a food processor, fit it with a steel blade and pulse until coarsely pureed. The last method to puree the soup is to use an immersion blender. (You can do that right in the soup pot). Return soup to the pot and re-heat. Add salt and pepper to taste. Serve hot. A last trick: use white pepper (again to taste) if you want to keep it a uniform creamy whitish color. (It may impress your guests).

Servings: 10. Preparation Time: 30 minutes (assuming beans are pre-soaked) Cooking Time: 1-2 hours.

Family Notes

Lentil Soup

I know, it's brown and thick and how are you going to get your kids to eat it, right? Even when I was young I balked at eating lentil soup too. I didn't care for the mushy yet firm consistency of the cooked lentil in the broth. Yet I have a couple of tricks which will get your kids over that hurdle. First, after you've cooked the soup, puree it with a stick blender or in a regular blender. Second add crispy pepperoni as a topping. The familiar and well-loved flavor of pepperoni, especially after it's been crisped helps sway those unwilling to try lentil soup. You merely need to add sliced pepperoni to a hot skillet for a couple minutes and they will curl up into cute little bowls as they cook.

Ingredients:
- 2 Tbsp. Olive Oil
- 2 – 3 Carrots, finely chopped
- 2- 3 Celery Stalks, finely chopped
- 1 Medium Onion, finely chopped
- 2 Tsp. Kosher Salt
- 1 Lb. Lentils, rinsed and cleaned
- 2 Quarts Chicken Stock (or Vegetable Stock)
- 1/2 Tsp, Ground Cumin
- 1 Pepperoni Stick (sliced thin—use as much as you like)

Procedure:
1. In a Dutch Oven, heat the olive oil and add the onions, carrots and celery. Cook till onions are translucent.

2. Add the lentils (some lentils need to be pre-soaked, check the package instructions) broth, salt and cumin. Stir and heat till nearly boiling. Lower heat and simmer for 45 minutes or until Lentils are tender.

3. Using an immersion blender, puree the lentils until smooth. Or transfer to a blender and puree. It may take two or three fillings. **Do not overfill the blender.** Heated liquid will expand and you will not have fun cleaning your kitchen. Return to the Dutch Oven and keep warm.

4. In a skillet heat your sliced pepperoni until they start to curl up. Ladle soup into bowls and add the sliced pepperoni 'cups' to the top. Serve.

Servings: 6 - 8. Preparation Time: 5 minutes. Cooking Time: 50 minutes.

Recipe Tip:
Lentils have been eaten for thousands of years all over the world and aside from soups are wonderful mixed with rice. They are high in protein, fiber, B vitamins and iron. If you use vegetable broth and skip the pepperoni, (add croutons instead) it's a balanced and wholesome vegetarian meal.

Family Notes

Fresh Minted Pea Soup

Pea Soup gets a bad rap because of its perceived consistency and color. People think it's mealy, gloppy and sometimes if it loses its brilliant green color it isn't palatable to look at either. The remedy to this is using a blender (or immersion blender if you have one) to whip the soup into shape! And of course adding fresh mint leaves takes away that baby-food connotation pea soup has.

Ingredients:
- 1 Tablespoon Olive Oil
- 1 Small Yellow Onion, peeled and medium diced
- ½ Teaspoon Salt
- ¼ Teaspoon Black Pepper
- 1 box frozen Peas, thawed
- 2/3 Cup Vegetable Stock
- Fresh Mint leaves, to taste

Procedure:
1. In a small sauté pan, or the Dutch Oven you'll use later, heat olive oil.
2. Add onions, salt and pepper and sauté until tender, but not brown, about 5 minutes.
3. Place the vegetable stock, peas, onions, and mint into a blender and process until desired consistency has been reached.
4. Pour soup into a 5 quart Dutch oven and simmer on medium-low for 20 minutes.
5. Serve.

Servings: 4 - 6. Preparation Time: 5 minutes. Cooking Time: 20 minutes.

Recipe Tips

Not all soups require hours of simmering and a laundry list of ingredients. This is one of a three which only need a half-hour and some fresh ingredients. We recommend pureeing many hearty soups simply to make them more palatable to younger kids.

Family Notes

Hot Parmesan-Tomato Soup

Tomato and parmesan is a classic taste combination and I don't know anyone who does not like it. When you use fresh ingredients and let them all meld together it becomes earthy, full flavored and very delicious. It's like a pizza but it's a soup.

Ingredients:
- 6oz. Plain Greek Yogurt
- 6 Vine Ripened Tomatoes, cut into quarters
- 1 Small Shallot, peeled
- Fresh Oregano, to taste
- Dried or Fresh Basil, to taste
- ¾ Cup Vegetable Stock
- 2 Tablespoons Sugar
- ¼ Teaspoon Black Pepper
- 2 Teaspoons of Worcestershire Sauce
- ½ Cup Grated Parmesan Cheese
- Fresh Thyme and Oregano, to taste and garnish

Procedure:
1. Place the first nine ingredients either into a blender. Or you can use a Dutch Oven or Soup pot and an immersion blender to puree.

2. If using a blender, blend all nine ingredients until desired consistency has been reached, then pour soup into a 5 quart soup pot or Dutch Oven. Bring the soup up to hot and check for seasoning. Add your cheese and fresh herbs and stir to combine simmer for 20 minutes then serve.

3. If using an immersion blender, you will obviously not need to transfer the soup to a pot. Bring soup up to hot, add cheese and fresh herbs, simmer for 20 minutes then serve.

Servings: 4 - 6. Preparation Time: 10 minutes. Cooking Time: 20 minutes.

Recipe Notes:
If you buy Parmesan Cheese with the rind still on it, save the rind! Freeze it, and the next time you are making any type of soup add the rind in and allow to cook with the soup. The rind will add tremendous flavor and it's a great way to reduce sodium in the recipe.

Family Notes

Chilled Agave Melon Soup

Fruit Soups are extremely popular in Europe and commonly served either hot or cold from Scandinavia down through Eastern Europe and into the Baltic regions. They generally use cream and dried fruits, especially so in the harsher climates.

Our soup is a little more Westernized because of the Agave and the melon. You can serve it as a starter course, or a mid day or evening snack. It's also fantastic for a summer time lunch because it's so cool and refreshing. Add a scoop or two of frozen yogurt or ice cream and the kids may not even know they're getting some wholesome fruit and necessary proteins.

Ingredients:
- 6oz. Plain Greek Yogurt
- ¾ Cup Milk
- 3 Tablespoons Agave Nectar
- 1 Small Cantaloupe, cut into chunks
- 3 Limes, juiced
- 1 -2 Tablespoons Fresh Mint

Procedure:
1. Place all ingredients into a blender in the order in which they are listed, and blend until desired consistency is reached.

2. Place in refrigerator for at least 30 minutes.

Servings: 4. Preparation Time: 5 minutes. Cooking Time: 30 minutes.

Family Notes

Tomato Corn Chowder

This is one zesty soup! The cream cheese provides a rich heartiness making this soup more of a chowder. It really works well all year round and is a great alternative to serving a chili on Super bowl Sunday. You can prepare it completely vegetarian too. You will find most of the ingredients already in your pantry, as they are the staples of any kitchen, so it is an economical meal.

Ingredients:
- 2 Tbsp Olive Oil
- ½ Cup Onions, finely chopped
- 1 tsp Each: Dried Oregano, Dried Thyme, Dried Basil
- ¼ tsp Celery Seed
- tsp Ground Cumin (always keep cumin on hand)
- ¼ tsp Each: Salt and Sugar
- 5 Grounds of Pepper (give the mill a good grind each time)
- 1 28oz. Can of Crushed Tomatoes (use a higher quality canned tomato)
- 2 lg. Fresh Tomatoes
- 1 ½ Cups Chicken or Vegetable Stock (low sodium)
- ¼ Cup Whole Wheat Pastry Flour
- 1 oz. Reduced Fat Cream Cheese (at room temperature)
- ¼ Cup 2% Milk (also can use Fat Free, Soy Milk or even water)
- 1 10oz. Box of Frozen Corn (or mixed vegetables)
- ½ cup Fresh Parsley (chopped)

Procedure
1. In a stockpot or cast iron enameled soup pot, heat olive oil on low setting. If you are using a stainless steel stock pot, be sure to use very low heat and your patience will allow a better sauté and no burning of the oil and herbs. Cast iron is a little more forgiving to higher temperatures. As the oil begins to heat, Toss in the onions, then the oregano, thyme, basil, (or if you have Italian blend herbs you can substitute for those three) celery seed, ¼ tsp cumin, ¼ salt, ¼ tsp sugar, and ground pepper. Sauté for about 5 minutes on med- low heat. This process really brings out the flavors and aromatics of the dried herbs. You will enjoy the smell in your kitchen. If you are using fresh herbs, double the amounts and use the same method.
2. Add the crushed tomatoes, 1 of the fresh tomatoes --chopped in large pieces, and 1 cup of stock. Mix to combine and cover the pot. Let simmer on low for 20 minutes, stirring occasionally.
3. While that is simmering, get a medium sized bowl and combine the flour, cream cheese and milk. This is a process you can have your kids do. Fold everything together.
4. You will need to temper the flour/cream cheese mixture to avoid curdling. Curdling won't ruin the food, but it won't look pretty. Ladle some of the soup into the flour/cream cheese bowl and mix to combine. Then add everything to the soup pot. Again, your kids can do this.
5. Add the corn, fresh parsley, 1 tsp cumin, and the second roughly chopped tomato, add salt, pepper and sugar to taste. Simmer for another 25 minutes, uncovered, and serve.
6. The sugar will cut down on the tomato's acidity. The cumin will provide a nice bit of smokey heat without the fire of chili peppers. And adding the second tomato at the end of the cooking cycle provides a bit of fresh vegetable to the soup.

Servings: 10. Preparation Time: 20 minutes. Cooking Time: 45 minutes.

Family Notes

Chapter 12
Snacks

Boneless Cheesy Chicken Tenders & Cool Blue Cheese Dip

You won't want to buy frozen or fast food chicken fingers after you try these. You control the salt content and the preservatives with natural condiments. These chicken tenders are juicy, meaty and delicious. A great healthy snack (they almost could be considered part of a meal) for the kids and the family to settle down with after school or on a weekend afternoon. They go especially well with the 'Cool Blue Cheese dressing' featured in our family favorite salad dressing section.

Ingredients:
- 1.5 Lbs. Chicken Tenders (or sliced chicken breasts)
- 1/4 Cup Red Hot Sauce (or as much as you can take)
- 4 Tbsp. Olive Oil
- ½ Cup Dijon Mustard
- 3 – 4 Tbsp. Honey
- ¾ Cup Bread Crumbs (Italian Style)
- 1¼ Cup Parmesan Cheese, grated

Procedure
1. Preheat your oven to 450 F Degrees.

2. In a large bowl, combine the hot sauce and olive oil with the mustard and honey. Stir. Add the chicken tenders and stir to coat evenly. Let stand for at least 30 minutes.

3. Get a pie dish or casserole and stir together the Parmesan cheese and the breadcrumbs. Take each chicken tender and dip in the breadcrumb mixture. Coat them completely and press to make sure the crumbs adhere well.

4. Transfer each piece to a cookie sheet lined with a Sil Pat or parchment paper. If you have neither, grease the sheet well with a light cooking or olive oil. Arrange evenly on the sheet, leaving some room between each chicken tender.

5. Bake for 12 – 15 minutes or until golden brown. (Time will depend on the size of the tenders).

Servings: 4. Preparation Time: 5 minutes. Inactive Time: 30 minutes. Cooking Time: 16 minutes.

Family Notes

Dani's Bean Dip

Isabella and her friend Danielle will make this as snack for themselves on weekends or when they get home from school. The ingredients are so common it's easy to keep them in your house thereby allowing you kids to make healthy snacking decisions. This snack is high in protein and fiber and has a decent fat content.

Ingredients:
- 1 Can Vegetarian Refried Beans
- 2 Tbsp Plain Greek Style Yogurt
- 2 – 3 Tbsp Salsa (any kind, any hotness)
- ¾ Cup Sharp Cheddar Cheese (shredded)

Procedure
1. Combine all ingredients in a medium sized stoneware bowl. Microwave for 35 seconds. Stir to mix in all the cheese before it gets too melted. Microwave for another 35 seconds. Serve with tortilla chips.

2. You can also serve this with cucumber slices, carrots and/or celery sticks.

Recipe Tip:
Use the Greek Style Yogurt because the protein to calorie ratio is superb! Greek Yogurt is usually twice as high in protein as regular yogurt. It tastes better too and does come in flavors. Buy it when it's on sale as it is more expensive than regular yogurt. Protein intake is critical to growing children (and adults too) and getting it from a low calorie source is key. Many of the fortified protein bars and snacks are very heavily sugared, processed and high in calories, making the potential to put on the wrong kind of weight (i.e. not lean muscle) highly likely.

Servings: 8. Preparation Time: 10 minutes.

Family Notes

First & Goal Fruit Dip

This is a side dish I like to put out when I have a bunch of kids around. It seems obvious but if you offer healthy snacks, hungry kids will eat them. Even at parties. Children will always gravitate to the candy and sugary treats, but I discovered that even if this dip were alongside the treats, it would get eaten as well. Toddlers do well with it if it's put on their plate with fruit or even graham crackers. There is about 2 grams of protein in 1 oz of cream cheese, which is very valuable to growing children. Plus, for busy parents it is extremely easy to make. No more difficult than combining a few ingredients and slicing seasonal fruits.

Ingredients:
- 8 oz of Reduced Fat Cream Cheese
- 1/3 Cup Packed Light Brown Sugar
- 1 Tbsp Pure Vanilla

Procedure

Combine together in a bowl and surround with a platter of fresh fruits.

Servings: 8. Preparation Time: 5 minutes.

Family Notes

Fruit Jell-O Surprise

OK I admit that I am a big kid at heart. I love Jell-O. I love making it, eating it, and playing with it. Jell-O is an underappreciated item, which I intend to bring back into our kitchens and meals. This Recipe is a real winner, and by using the V-8 Fruit Fusion juice you are really boosting up your kids intake of fruits and vegetables without them even knowing it. If you try nothing else in this book, you have to try this. Get your kids involved and have a great time together.

Ingredients:
- 13 oz. Package of your favorite flavor of Jell-O (I like Mixed berry)
- 3 oz. Packages of unflavored Gelatin (usually available in 1 oz. packets)
- 2 Cups 100% Fruit Juice (flavor should be similar to Jell-O)
- 2 Cups Cold Water
- 1 Large Apple (or 2 medium ones), sliced into ¼ inch thick rounds.

Procedure
1. In a large bowl or 4 cup measuring glass, combine the Jell-O and Gelatin, whisk to combine.
2. In a small sauce pan bring to a boil 2 cups fruit juice.
3. Add the hot fruit juice to the Jell-O mixture, and stir with a silicone spoon until Jell-O and gelatin are completely dissolved.
4. Add 2 cups cold water, mix to combine.
5. Using a 9 x 13 glass baker, pour ½ the Jell-O liquid into the baker and refrigerate for 25-30 minutes.
6. Meanwhile slice the apple(s) into ¼"rounds using a cookie cutter about 1 to 1.5" in diameter cut out 6 centers of apple. (No needs to peel apple(s) as you are using the center of each slice.
7. Pull Jell-O out of refrigerator and place apple slices evenly apart on top of first layer, then pour remaining liquid Jell-O over them. Refrigerate until completely set, about 1 hour.
8. Remove from refrigerator and cut out shapes with a 2" or 3 inch cookie cutter.

Servings: 8. Preparation Time: 15 minutes. Inactive Time: 1 hour.

Recipe Tips
I use an offset spatula to remove the excess Jell-O away from the cookie cutter, and then slide the spatula underneath the cookie cutter and Jell-O to lift out.

Apple slices may float to top that is fine, and as you put the dish back into the refrigerator they may move around, just settle the dish in the fridge, and move the slices with your finger back into place. Also allow Jell-O to fully set. Save the excess Jell-O for snacks later with some Whip Cream.

These can be made 2 days ahead and stored in a plastic container with wax paper in between each Jell-O Cut out.

Family Notes

Hike and Go Trail Mix

This mix will keep your kids interested and they will always be happy to take it along on a hike or family trip. This granola/trail mix is perfect alongside a glass of milk or added to a bowl of hot or cold cereal. I like to make large batches because its stores so well. Feel free to double on the ingredient amounts. It's less expensive than buying store made granola too. It's a great 'bus stop' breakfast snack too for those teens just too busy to sit and eat in the morning. You won't need to bring a bag of chips to the game or for the car ride, either.

Ingredients:
- 1 Cup Oatmeal
- 1 Cup Dried Fruit (of your choice)
- 1 Cup Nuts (of your choice)
- 1 Cup Light Brown Sugar, packed
- 1/8- 1/4 Tsp. Cayenne (optional)

Procedure
1. Coat the first 3 ingredients with the light brown sugar and cayenne pepper (if using) and spread the mix out a baking sheet lined with a Sil Pat or Parchment paper. Pour the mixture evenly over the covered baking sheet. Bake in a pre-heated 350 F degree oven for 15 – 20 minutes, until golden brown. As it cooks, the sugar will melt and then harden over the mix making a nice coating.

2. Allow to cool. Store in an airtight container until ready to use.

Servings: 8. Preparation Time: 5 minutes Cooking Time: 20 minutes.

Family Notes

Mackenzie's Grandma's Great Granola

This recipe comes from the Kitchen of Mackenzie's Grandma Dot. Mackenzie is featured in many of our cooking segments and she shared this recipe with us. Aside from using a hot oven, any school age kid can do it. This makes a total of 8 Cups of granola, which makes it very cost effective.

Ingredients:

- 3 Cups Quick Oats (uncooked)
- 1 ½ Cup Chopped Walnuts (optional)
- 1 Cup Coconut
- ½ Cup Butter Melted (a ½ cup equals 1 stick)
- 1/3 Cup Local Honey
- 1 ½ Cups Raisins

Procedure

1. Mix the first 5 ingredients until moistened. Spread out onto an ungreased cookie sheets. Bake 10 minutes at 350 degrees F.

2. Let cool and serve or parcel out into sealable bags or containers.

3. If the mixture seems too dry, add a little water and extend the cooking time a few minutes. You will need a little liquid if you are adding ingredients or doubling the recipe.

Servings: 6. Preparation Time: 10 minutes. Cooking Time: 10 minutes.

Recipe Tip:

You can add other ingredients such as Wheat Germ, (sprinkle in a generous amount with the Oatmeal.) Instead of, or along with, raisins add dried fruits like cranberries, chopped apricots or chopped dates. Chocolate chips are good too. Just put them in at the end, unless you want to melt chocolate over the fruit and nuts.

Both the *'Hike and Go Trail Mix'* and *'Grandma's Great Granola'* are excellent ways to fortify morning cereals with natural and wholesome, nutrient rich ingredients. I add a large spoonful or two it my oatmeal every morning.

Family Notes

My Mom's Famous Pumpernickel Bread Dip

You have all seen it. It is this very dark round mass with a creamy white center that has probably sat on every buffet and kitchen island for the last 40 odd years. It is a party mainstay and everybody has a variation of it. It has most likely scared children away because of how it looks. "Oh No! There must be vegetables in this! I'm not going near it!" they say in their minds. So, I say get your children to make this with you. It is so easy they can actually do it themselves. And look Mom, no vegetables! As far as hors d'ouvers are concerned, this is really not a bad thing to snack on. We're using reduced fat mayo and sour cream and pumpernickel bread has a lot of nutritional value. My mother has been making this dip since before I was born. The secret is the Beau-Monde Seasoning, which is a proprietary blend of multiple spices including celery, onion, bay, allspice and salt. Buying a bottle won't go to waste just for this dip. You can add this spice to a variety of dips, roasts (beef and fowl), salads, and when you sauté leafy green vegetables. Also try to get a genuine Pumpernickel loaf if you can. You'll know its genuine because the ingredient list will state mostly Rye grain. It's not the end of the world if you can't find one the Mass produced loaves work, and are so prevalent most Americans would not know there is actually a difference.

Ingredients:
- 1 ½ Cups Reduced Fat Real Mayonnaise
- 1 ½ Cups Reduced Fat Sour Cream
- 1 Tbsp. Beau-Monde Seasoning (Spice Islands brand)
- 1 ½ Tsp. Fresh Dill
- 1 ½ Tsp. Fresh Flat Leaf Parsley (chopped)
- 1 Large Round Loaf of Pumpernickel Bread (not sliced)

Procedure
1. Combine all ingredients (except the bread) in a bowl and refrigerate for at least a few hours if not overnight.

2. To Serve: It couldn't be simpler. Hollow out a well in the loaf of the Pumpernickel. This is easy if you just cut an opening in the top. The crust is very thin. Then pull out the center of the bread, getting as much as possible. Continue to hollow out the interior until you have enough bread. You will need to tear the bread into pieces to use for dipping. Again your kids can do all of this -- leaving you time to do other things. They might like it. (Just remind them to wash their hands). Set the hollowed out loaf on a platter and put the bread pieces around it. Fill the center with the dip.

Servings: 10. Preparation Time: 5 minutes. Inactive Time: 1 hour.

Family Notes

Pretzels

I miss the pretzels you get from the snack carts in New York City. They seem to have a special taste and are warm and comforting. Connecticut just does not have those street vendors. My pretzel recipe makes nice big, bready pretzels, hinted with salt, delicious and so effortless to make at home. It's a perfect recipe for kids of any age to make on their own or assist with.

These are not the dry crunchy pieces of tree branches that you get in cellophane bags either. Pair them up with any kind of mustard whether sweet, spicy or hot and you can have yourself a great sports party or the perfect movie snack for the entire family. This recipe makes 16 pretzels. They are best when fresh —but don't worry they will be gone quickly.

Ingredients:
- 1 Envelope Active Dry Yeast
- 1 1/2 Cups Very Warm Water
- 1 Tablespoon Sugar
- 2 Tsp. Salt
- 4 Cups Whole Wheat Pastry Flour
- 1 Egg Yolk
- 1 Tablespoon Water
- 1/4 Cup Coarse Salt

Procedure:
1. Dissolve Yeast in a bowl containing the cup of warm water (110 degrees).
2. Stir in Sugar and Salt until dissolved. Add Flour and mix well.
3. Turn out dough onto a floured surface and knead for 5 minutes.
4. Divide Dough in 16 equal pieces.
5. Roll into thin strips and shape into pretzels, then place on a well greased baking sheet.
6. Beat an egg yolk with a little water and brush the tops of each pretzel.
7. Sprinkle with the Coarse Salt.
8. Bake at 425 degrees F, for 15 to 20 minutes.

Servings: 16. Preparation Time: 15 minutes. Cooking Time: 20 minutes.

Family Notes

Michelle's Twisted Peanut Butter and Apples

As a child, and still today as an adult, my favorite snack is Peanut Butter and Apples. I eat it all the time. This version is a twist on an old favorite. It is simple and quick, and the Peanut Butter mixture can be made in advance and stored at room temperature in a Tupperware container.

Ingredients:
- Reduced Fat Peanut Butter, 1 Cup
- ¼ Cup Local Honey
- 1 Tsp. Cinnamon
- Apples, (variety of your liking) cored and cut into wedges

Procedure
1. Combine the Peanut Butter, Honey, and Cinnamon in a container
2. Core the Apples, then slice into thick wedges
3. Spread the peanut butter mixture onto each wedge and enjoy!

Servings: 4. Preparation Time: 5 minutes.

Recipe Tips
You can make as much or as little of the Peanut Butter mixture, by increasing or decreasing the amounts proportionately. You can use the mixture as a dip too.

There is plenty of nutrition in this snack. For comparison sake, Peanut Butter has fewer calories (1tablespoon equals approximately 90 calories, varies by brand) than Olive Oil yet it has all the same healthy fats and (again varies by brand) 3 to 4 grams of protein.

Cinnamon is much more than one of the world's most popular spices. Real cinnamon's essential oils are extremely high in antioxidants and are anti microbial which can inhibit bacterial growth in some foods. It has been reported to have remarkable pharmacological effects too. It was used to treat wounds in the ancient world. New studies are being done about its effectiveness in the treatment of arthritis, diabetes, cancer and as a digestive aid.

Family Notes

Chapter 13
Sweet Treats

Butter Pecan Turtle Cookies

Growing up my mom played a large part in developing my love for cooking. I always looked forward to getting in the kitchen and cooking with her. These Cookies have been a holiday favorite since I was six or seven. My mom would always make them and everyone who had one could never get enough. These may not be considered nutritious, but they taste great and are a lot more fun to make (and less expensive) than to go out and buy.

Ingredients for the Crust:
- 2 Cups Flour
- 1 Cup Firmly Packed Brown Sugar
- ½ Cup Butter, softened

Ingredients for Caramel Layer:
- 2/3 Cups Butter
- ½ Cup Firmly Packed Brown Sugar

Topping:
- 1 Cup Milk Chocolate Chips
- 1 Cup Whole Pecan Halves

Procedure
1. Pre-heat oven to 350 F degrees

2. In a 3qt. Stand Mixer, or by hand, mix crust ingredients at medium speed until well mixed and particles are fine. Pat mixture into a 9x13 pan. Sprinkle whole pecans over unbaked crust.

3. In a large saucepan, combine butter and sugar over a medium heat, stirring constantly, until entire surface of mixture begins to boil for 30 seconds pour mixture over nuts and crust.

4. Bake in the center of your oven for 18-22 minutes. Remove from oven, sprinkle with chips, swirl chips and let cool.

Servings: 24. Preparation Time: 10 minutes. Cooking Time: 20 minutes.

Family Notes

Carrot Cake

This is my Mom's Carrot Cake recipe and it is definitely NOT your average Carrot Cake! The first big difference is there is no Cream Cheese Frosting, which truthfully, I am not a fan of. The taste of this cake is unlike any other, the glaze sinks down into it while still warm. It is truly wonderful; you and your kids will enjoy this recipe for years to come. It makes a lot- so let the kids bring over some friends, or bring this to your next family event. Either way, don't expect any to be left over.

Ingredients:
- 2 Cups Flour
- 1 Tsp. Baking Soda
- 2 Tsp Salt
- 1 ½ Cups Sugar
- 2 Tsp Cinnamon
- 3 Large Eggs
- ¾ Cup Buttermilk
- ½ Cup Vegetable Oil
- 1 Tbs. Vanilla
- 1 1/8 Cups Crushed Pineapple
- 2 Cups Carrots, Finely grated (and liquid squeezed out)
- 1 Cup Coarsely Chopped Nuts (optional)
- 1 Cup Coconut (optional)

Glaze:
- 2/3 Cup Sugar
- ¼ Tsp. Baking Soda
- 1/3 Cup Buttermilk

Procedure
1. Preheat oven 350 F degrees
2. Sift flour, baking powder, salt, sugar, and cinnamon.
3. Beat eggs with buttermilk, oil and vanilla.
4. Add wet ingredients all at once to dry, mix until smooth. Fold in Pineapple, carrots, nuts and coconut. Pour into greased 9x13" pan. Bake for 45 minutes or until center sprigs back.
5. Combine all Glaze ingredients in a saucepan and heat until sugar is dissolved.
6. When the cake comes out of the oven, use a fork to poke holes all over the cake. Then pour the warm glaze over it so that the glaze soaks deep into the cake.

Servings: 12. Preparation Time: 5 minutes. Cooking Time: 45 minutes.

Family Notes

Fantastic Flourless Brownies (Gluten- Free)

These brownies use NO FLOUR! They are quick to make, very moist and fudgy, use few ingredients, and only requires an oven, baking dish and a food processor. Here's a dish you may want to make for the kids when they ARE NOT around. I know we encourage kids to work with parents, but when they see a can of Black Beans going in the batter (or in this case being the batter) they may not go near it. But I defy anybody who doesn't know the recipe to figure out there is no flour! Plus, these brownies are packed with protein so kids will get a lot of good, energy-boosting nutrition. It's a great snack for your teenage boys to eat when they come home from sports. **If you are concerned about gluten- free eating follow the recipe closely and use gluten free chocolate chips.** If not, don't worry about the gluten free ingredients. A couple of other things; you can mix the chips to your taste from semi-sweet to bittersweet in any combination. A drizzle of chocolate on top of the brownies makes a nice presentation too.

Ingredients:
- 1 (15 ounce) Can No-Salt or Low Sodium Black Beans, drained & rinsed
- 3 Large Eggs
- 1/3 Cup melted Butter, (and enough to coat baking dish)
- ½ Cup high quality Cocoa Powder
- 1/8 Teaspoon salt (use only if using no-salt black beans, otherwise eliminate)
- 2 Teaspoons **Gluten-Free**, Real Vanilla Extract
- ½ Cup plus 2 tablespoons Cane Sugar (also called Florida Crystals)
- 1 Cup **Gluten-Free** Semi-Sweet Chocolate Chips
- 1/3 Cup finely chopped Walnuts (optional)

Procedure
1. Butter an 8-inch baking pan and preheat oven to 350 degrees F.

2. To get the consistency right you will need a food processor for this recipe. Combine all the ingredients-- except the chocolate chips and nuts—in the food processor bowl. Blend into a smooth consistency. Remove the blade and carefully fold in the chocolate chips and the walnuts. Pour mixture in the buttered baking dish. You will need to bake the brownies for 30 to 35 minutes or until a toothpick comes clean from the center.

Servings: 6. Preparation Time: 10 minutes. Cooking Time: 30 minutes.

Recipe Tips
The more you puree the black beans in the food processor the better these are, you really want to make sure the skins of the black beans are well broken down and not noticeable when eaten.

Since the list is very simple, I recommend getting the highest quality cocoa powder and vanilla extract you can find.

Family Notes

Individual Apple Dumplings

Apple dumplings have had a long history in the United States, and almost every culture has brought over their own version. This recipe reminds me of my mother's kitchen, which brings back such warm happy memories for me. This recipe is a memory waiting to be made with your child. This is fun and easy. When your child is grown, they will have that same happy feeling as I do whenever they make these Apple Dumplings.

Ingredients:
- ¼ Cup Dried Cranberries
- 3 Tbsp. Pecans, finely chopped (any nuts of your choice will work)
- 1 Tbsp Cinnamon
- ¼ tsp. Nutmeg
- 1/8 tsp. Cloves
- ¼ Cup Local Honey
- ¼ Cup Boiling Water
- 2 Granny Smith Apples, halved and cored
- 1 Package Pie Crust (usually 2 in a box)
- 1 Tbsp. Honey, microwaved for 10 –15 seconds for topping of the wrapped apples.

Procedure
1. Preheat Oven to 375 F degrees
2. In a medium bowl combine all ingredients except the apples and dough, allow to sit for 10 minutes.
3. Peel the apples, cut each in half length wise, using a teaspoon, or melon baller, scoop out the core, making a large hole, do not go all the way through the apple.
4. Spoon mixture into all 4 apple halves.
5. Divide the first of 2 pie dough's into 2 parts, wrap each piece of dough around each apple half, encasing the entire half in dough, seal well at bottom of apple, and place seam side down in to a baking dish, when all apples are wrapped and in the baking dish, brush the tops of each apple with a Tbsp of honey that's been microwaved in a separate bowl for 10-15 seconds.
6. Place the apples into the oven and bake for 35 minutes.
7. Serve warm with some frozen vanilla yogurt or at room temp.

Servings: 4. Preparation Time: 20 minutes. Cooking Time: 35 minutes.

Family Notes

Individual Fruit Ambrosia

I grew up making this dessert every holiday with my Mom and Aunt Rachel. It just seems so grown up to a young child. I absolutely love this dessert, you can make a bigger version in a trifle bowl for your entire family, or your kids can make their own smaller version. This dessert is best made ahead and allowed to marinate in the refrigerator for a few hours. Also this dessert freezes really well, so you can have the kids help you make it, then store in the freezer, and pull out as needed.

Ingredients:
- 1 Can Fruit Cocktail, drained
- 8 oz. Sour Cream (Reduced Fat)
- 1 Apple, peeled and diced
- 1 Bag Frozen Mixed Berries, defrosted
- 1 Can Mandarin Oranges, drained
- 1 Cup Mini Marshmallows
- 1 Cup Coconut
- 6 Ramekins (or other suitable dessert vessel)

Procedure

Layer each ramekin in the following sequence:
1. About 1 Tablespoon of Fruit Cocktail, Apples, a few of the defrosted Berries, Mandarin Oranges, Sour Cream, Marshmallows, and the Coconut.
- Repeat a second time. Refrigerate until ready to serve. You can substitute whatever fruit suits your family's taste.

Servings: 6. Preparation Time: 10 minutes. Inactive Time: 1 hour.

Family Notes

My Mom's Apple Pie

Nothing conjures up American home cooking like the smell of my Apple Pie. My mom's is so good— not too sweet or too tart because of the mix of apples. Her secret is in the Tapioca, which acts as a thickener. Rather than using flour or cornstarch, I use Tapioca in all my fruit pies and believe me it makes a HUGE difference. People will want to know what your secret is, and you can tell them, or just smile and say nothing.

Ingredients:

- 6 Cups Apples, peeled, cored and sliced thin (use a mix: Granny Smith, Cortland, Macoun)
- 2 Tbs. Kraft Minute Tapioca
- 1/3 Cup white sugar
- 1/3 Cup Brown Sugar, packed
- ½ Tsp. Cinnamon
- 1/8 Tsp Nutmeg
- ½ Lemon, squeezed
- 1 Package of Refrigerated Pie Crust
- 1 Large Egg, mixed with a 2 Tbsp. Cream, set aside
- 1 Tbs. Unsalted Butter

Procedure

1. Preheat Oven to 400 F degrees
2. Mix first 6 ingredients together let stand at least 15 minutes.
3. While the apples sit, roll out the first pie dough and fit into a 9 inch pie dish. Using a pastry brush coat the bottom and sides of the dough with some of the egg and cream mixture, this will prevent getting a soggy bottom crust.
4. Pour Apple mixture into prepared pie dish, using your hands push down on the apples, ensuring that there is little to no space in between the apples, this helps to keep your apple pie from collapsing while baking.
5. Dot the top with a bit of unsalted butter, then roll out the 2nd crust and place on top of pie, tuck the edges into the side of the pie dish to help seal in the juices.
6. Cut slits into the top of the pie, to allow steam to escape.
7. Take the egg and cream mixture and brush the top of the pie, then sprinkle with a bit of sugar.
8. Bake for 50 to 1 hour. Let rest for 30 minutes before serving.

Servings: 8. Preparation Time: 1 hour. Cooking Time: 1 hour.

Recipe Tips

I like to throw in 2-3 sweeter apples into the mix this helps balance the tartness of the Granny Smith Apples without having to add a lot of sugar to your pie.

Also I have used a refrigerated pie crust in this recipe for fast easy pie assembly, but if you have a homemade pie dough recipe by all means use it.

Family Notes

Stone Fruit Tart

Every summer Elisabeth's grandmother used to make this tart using those Italian Prune Plums, the small egg shaped bluish- purple ones with the yellowy flesh. They can hard to find due to a short growing season. Use whatever abundant fruit you might have on hand. This works well with pears, apples, peaches, or whatever stone fruit is in season. The prune plum is an especially great plum for cooking or baking with because the pits are easily removed and they turn fuchsia when cooked. Just remember to use plums that are not quite ripe—otherwise your pie crust will get too soggy. If you like a gooey plum crumble, don't worry about it.

We are using Pears in this recipe which impart a wonderful sweetness to the tart. I use a pre-made pie crust when I don't have time to make one from scratch. This way I put together a quick desert after work --or the kids can make a healthy snack when they come from school with unexpected friends.

Ingredients:
- 1 Pre-Packaged Pie Dough
- 1 Egg Yolk
- 1 Tbsp of Tapioca (per pound of fruit)
- 9 or 10 pieces of Fruit, sliced or halved (depending on what fruit and how much you have and how much you want to put on the top of the tart.)
- 1/4 Teaspoon Ground Cinnamon
- ¼ Cup White Sugar
- ¼ Cup Brown Sugar
- 1 Egg and 1 Tbsp Water (to make an egg wash)

Procedure
1. Preheat your oven to 400 F degrees
2. Roll out prepared Pie dough on to a Sil Pat or Piece of Parchment paper. Brush the egg yolk over the pie dough, then transfer to a half sheet pan.
3. Combine fruit, tapioca, cinnamon, sugar, and sprinkle over the fruit. Let the fruit sit for 15 minutes, then Pour Fruit Mixture in the center of your Pie Dough, leaving a 1-2" edge all the way around, wrap the edges of the dough around the fruit, glaze the edges with either an egg wash or cream, and sprinkle with sugar. Bake between 20 and 30 minutes. Visually you will see that the crust is golden, and the fruit has softened.

Servings: 6. Preparation Time: 15 minutes. Cooking Time: 30 minutes.

Family Notes

Sum 'or Turnovers

What kid does not love S'Mores? For that matter what adult does not love them? I created this late one night. I had a craving for something warm, gooey, and decadent, and these are what I came up with. Enjoy them, I know I do.

Plus the kids will enjoy crushing up the graham crackers. It gives them something fun to "destroy".

Ingredients:
- 1 Package of Refrigerator Pie Crust (15 oz.)
- 1 Cup Chocolate Chips
- 1 Cup Mini Marshmallows
- 10 Cinnamon Graham Crackers, Crushed
- 1 Tbs. Cinnamon Sugar
- 1 Large Egg, Beaten

Procedure
1. Preheat Oven to 325 F Degrees.
2. Unfold the Pie Crust and cut into 4 pieces.
3. Put a few chocolate chips and a few marshmallows in the center of each dough piece, fold each dough piece into a triangle, and using a fork, crimp the edges to seal in the chocolate and marshmallows.
4. Place the turnovers onto an ungreased cookie sheet.
5. Using a pastry brush, brush the egg wash onto each turnover, then sprinkle the tops of each with the graham crackers and cinnamon sugar.

Servings: 4. Preparation Time: 5 minutes. Cooking Time: 25 minutes.

Family Notes

Index

Families are like recipes. Individual ingredients are not necessarily dynamic enough to make a great meal. They need to be brought together.

Michelle Day

Michelle Day has been cooking and baking since she was old enough to hold a whisk. Michelle credits her parents with her love for cooking which set her on the path to make a career out of baking, preparing and devising catering menus and teaching culinary programs. In her career, she started a successful catering business on New York City's Upper East and has been able to incorporate her love of baking by designing beautiful and artistic cakes for clients and special events. Michelle has years of culinary experience managing a premiere gourmet food and equipment retailer and has taught extremely popular children and family oriented cooking classes. She has a list of clients clamoring for her next event or customized cake design. She has made appearances on television, and at special events, and regularly teaches culinary classes throughout Connecticut.

Eric Bleimeister

Has been an enthusiastic cook since he moved out of his parent's home. He remembers how his mother served a hearty dinner every night when his father came home from work. These solid memories of family life around the dinner table stick with him today. Eric has over 20 years experience with fitness, nutrition and writing. He loves cooking and has always been called upon to whip up main courses for every social occasion and continually comes to the rescue of overworked friends. Whether it's on the grill, the stovetop or in the oven, Eric's has an inherent savvy of how to mix ingredients together and make a delicious meal.

He is the parent of a finicky eater and this challenge—to get his child to eat well in a world of pre-packaged and sugary foods-- has inspired him to write this book with Michelle. 'Kids and a Cook' has given him opportunity to combine both is passions and start a career as a food writer.

'Kids and a Cook' also features an energetic, precocious 9-year-old named **Elisabeth Bleimeister**. Although a finicky eater, Elisabeth still loves to cook in the kitchen and learn about ingredients and how to mix them to make tasty dishes.
Log onto kids and a cook. com for more recipes and food information